D. K. Flickinger

Ethiopia - Twenty-Six Years of Missionary Life in Western Africa:

With an appendix embracing the period between 1877 and 1882

D. K. Flickinger

Ethiopia - Twenty-Six Years of Missionary Life in Western Africa:
With an appendix embracing the period between 1877 and 1882

ISBN/EAN: 9783743355217

Manufactured in Europe, USA, Canada, Australia, Japa

Cover: Foto ©ninafisch / pixelio.de

Manufactured and distributed by brebook publishing software (www.brebook.com)

D. K. Flickinger

Ethiopia - Twenty-Six Years of Missionary Life in Western Africa:

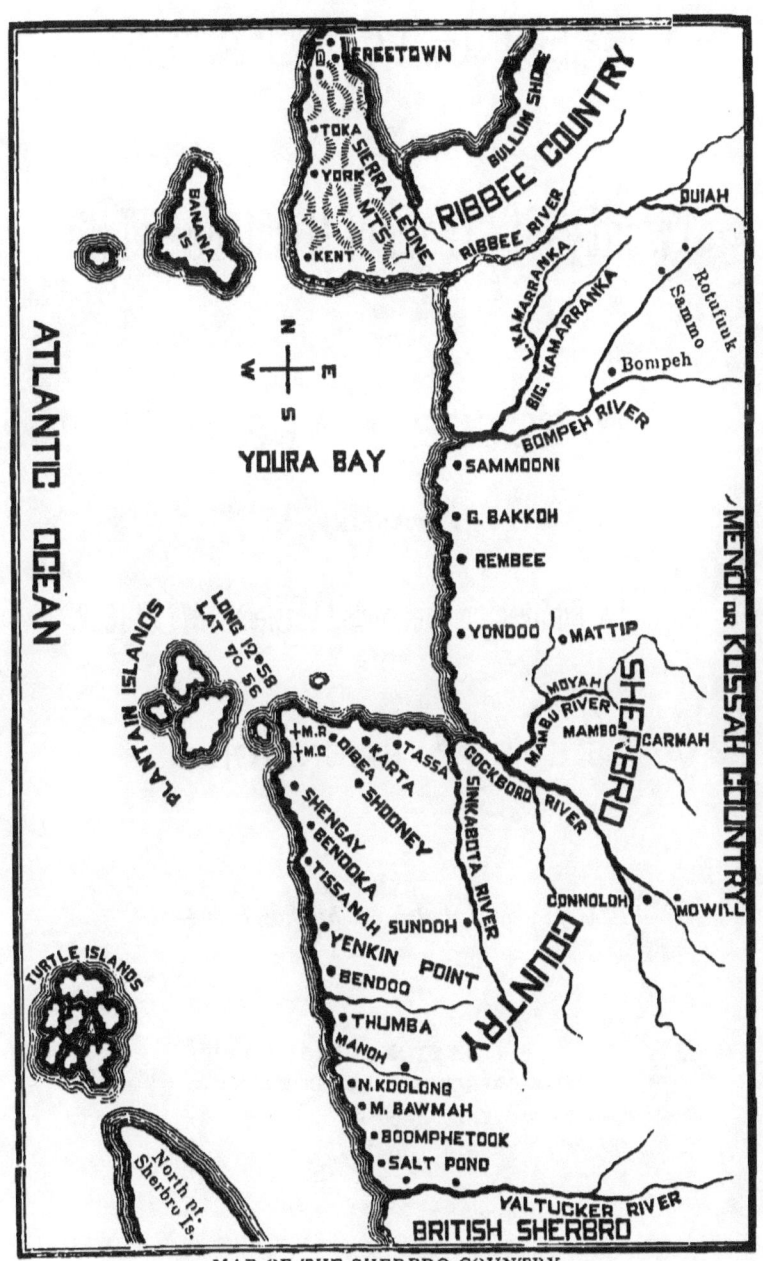

MAP OF THE SHERBRO COUNTRY.

ETHIOPIA;

OR,

Twenty-Six Years of Missionary Life

IN

WESTERN AFRICA,

WITH AN

Appendix Embracing the Period between 1877 & 1882.

BY

REV. D. K. FLICKINGER.

"Ethiopia shall stretch out her hands to God."

DAYTON, OHIO:
UNITED BRETHREN PUBLISHING HOUSE.
1882.

BOOK COMMITTEE'S RECOMMENDATION.

The undersigned having examined the manuscript copy of a book written by Rev. D. K. Flickinger, entitled, "Ethiopia; or, Twenty Years of Missionary life in Western Africa," do hereby approve its publication, and recommend it to the favor of the people of the Church of the United Brethren in Christ.

D. BERGER,
J. W. HOTT,
W. O. TOBEY,
WM. MITTENDORF.
} Book Committee.

Dayton, Ohio, July 10, 1877.

Entered according to act of Congress, in the year 1877,
BY REV. W. J. SHUEY,
In the office of the Librarian of Congress, at Washington, D. C.

STEREOTYPED AT THE
UNITED BRETHREN PRINTING HOUSE,
DAYTON, OHIO.

INDORSEMENT.

FROM REV. J. K. BILLHEIMER.

The fact that the author has been for twenty years corresponding secretary of the Home, Frontier, and Foreign Missionary Society of the Church of the United Brethren in Christ, is sufficient to recommend these pages. In this relation he has acquired, by personal visitation, a complete knowledge of its missionary operations throughout the Church. He knows the African mission intimately from the beginning. Others have spent more time in that country, but his official connection with the mission has remained unbroken from the time it was projected to the present; and four times has he crossed the ocean, giving his personal service to that work for from one half to one and a half years each time.

In this volume he makes no attempt at theories or probabilities, but gives us an interesting sketch of the people and their customs and habits, and of mission-life among them. I feel confident that the circulation of this volume will awaken many latent hearts to sympathy with the mission. Respectfully.

J. K. BILLHEIMER.

Dayton, Ohio, August 1, 1877.

FROM REV. JOSEPH GOMER.

Having examined carefully the manuscript pages of "Ethiopia; or, Twenty Years of Missionary Life in Western Africa." I take great pleasure in certifying to the correctness of its delineations of the country, its inhabitants, and their modes of life. The brief and vivid method the author has adopted in treating his subjects will add greatly to the interest of the book, and especially will his history of Sherbro Mission prove a highly valuable part of the volume

JOSEPH GOMER.

PREFACE.

Twenty years ago a small book, entitled "Off-Hand Sketches in Africa," was written and published by the author of the present volume. It received sufficient favor to justify the issuing of several editions. Most of the matter contained in that volume, thoroughly revised, and with material additions, has been transferred to the pages of the present book. Other portions of the book, especially some of the letters from missionaries in Africa, and the notes from the journal of one of their number, are now for the first time given to the public. These portions will be found valuable as aiding in giving a connected history of Sherbro Mission. The illustrations of African scenery, implements, and so on, with a single exception, are engraved from original photographs, as are also those of the persons represented, and may be relied on as being essentially correct. The map of the Sherbro country and adjacent regions, engraved especially for this book, will be found valuable. Rev. J. K. Billheimer, who is familiar with the country, testifies to its essential accuracy. The book is sent forth with a sincere desire that by contributing to the increase of knowledge of western Africa and the condition of its people, it may aid in awakening Christian sympathy and stimulating effort for the deliverance of millions from the night and chains of heathenism.

D. K. FLICKINGER.

INTRODUCTION.

If intimate acquaintance with the facts to be presented and an intensified interest in the subject to be treated constitute any part of the essentials requisite for authorship, then the writer of the following pages may lay more than ordinary claims to this qualification. At four different times he crossed the ocean to visit the lands and the people of which he writes the first voyage being made some twenty-two years ago. Since then the mission at that time organized has occupied, his unceasing thought and care, and no other man is so intimately acquainted as he with its history through all the stages of its development to the present time. Mr. Flickinger has long cultivated habits of close observation, and when traveling is thoroughly wakeful to everything that transpires about him. His sketches of the people of western Africa, of their habits, customs, modes of life, superstitions, and idolatries, are drawn from notes made on the ground. His ability to acquire so close a knowledge of African life was largely gained through the influence his official position secured for him with the native African chiefs. The sketches are vividly drawn, and frequently give us in the fewest words

CONTENTS.

Chapter.		Page.
XXXIII.	What justice demands, God commands	119
XXXIV.	Measure and test of love	119
XXXV.	What the Gospel will do	127
XXXVI.	Location of Sherbro Mission	122
XXXVII.	Shengay Mission-Station	136
XXXVIII.	Dr. Witt and Rev. J. A. Williams	140
XXXIX.	Religious awakening, first converts	142
XL.	What was done from 1860 to 1870,	146
XLI.	Mr. Gomer and wife and Mr. Evans sent to Africa, Mrs. Hadley's return	154
XLII.	Another chapel needed, appointment of Mr. Warner and wife	159
XLIII.	How two chiefs who were at enmity became reconciled	161
XLIV.	Missionaries coming from and going to Africa, Industrial School	163
XLV.	Rev. J. A. Evans	166
XLVI.	Extracts from Rev. J. Gomer's journal	167
XLVII.	Letters written by missionaries	180
XLVIII.	What we can and ought to have, soon, in Africa,	237
XLVIX.	Letters from Missionaries	241

MISSIONARY LIFE IN WESTERN AFRICA.

CHAPTER I.

THE COUNTRY AND PEOPLE.

On the west coast of Africa, and immediately south and south-east of the colony of Sierra Leone, are the country and people of which I shall write, with the distinct understanding that what I shall say of the people will relate to those tribes visited by me in my sojournings in that country, namely, the Mendi, Sherbro, and Timiny tribes.

In Africa, as in other heathen countries similarly governed, tribes living adjacent to each other are materially unlike in their customs and habits, as also in respect to moral character, some having sunk much lower in vice than others; and this accounts, in part, for the seemingly conflicting statements of missionaries who have visited that country.

INTRODUCTION.

strikingly distinct impressions of the scenes described or the facts stated. The copious extracts from the letters of missionaries now in the field, and of others who have served there in other years, as also the notes from the journal of one of the principal missionaries, form an interesting and valuable part of the book. In this correspondence indeed will be found, incidentally, drawn from strictly original sources, an instructive portion of the history of the mission. The history, by means of these letters, is brought down to the present time.

Having read carefully these pages in the proof-sheets, I take the sincerest pleasure in commending the book to the good will of others. The general reader will find it highly interesting and profitable. And especially do I recommend it to the favor of those having the care of Sabbath-schools as a book eminently suited to the requirements of the library, and adapted to the instruction of the young.

DANIEL BERGER.

CONTENTS.

CHAPTER.		PAGE.
I.	The country and people	9
II.	Towns, locality and description	11
III.	Houses, how furnished	13
IV.	Barras	15
V.	Food	17
VI.	Cooking, eating, bathing	19
VII.	Dress	22
VIII.	Their sleeping fixtures	24
IX.	Labor, farming, manufactures, trades	26
X.	War	31
XI.	Amusements	32
XII.	Their physical structure	35
XIII.	Dispositions, taste for music	38
XIV.	Deceptions	40
XV.	Evangelization, its difficulties	43
XVI.	Languages	46
XVII.	Marking time, counting, etc	48
XVIII.	Etiquette	52
XIX.	Ancient customs	55
XX.	Laws, government	57
XXI.	Oaths, currency	60
XXII.	Matrimony, abuse of women	62
XXIII.	Funeral ceremonies, witchcraft	70
XXIV.	Theology, devil-worship	76
XXV.	Gregrees	81
XXVI.	Creation of man	89
XXVII.	Future state	92
XXVIII.	Slavery, slave-trade	95
XXIX.	Purrow-bush society	100
XXX.	Condition and wants of the people	104
XXXI.	Encouragements to labor	106
XXXII.	The vicious influence of the whites	111

Below the Sierra Leone mountains, and immediately on the coast, the country is low and marshy, and much of it is inundated with water when the streams are highest during the rainy season. The country is thickly interspersed with rivers, many of which are mere tide-water streams in the dry season; or at most, above the point where the tide ceases to affect them they dwindle down to small creeks and rivulets.

The principal timber of the lowlands is the mangrove-tree. A little of other kinds, such as bamboo, palm, cotton, and so on, is to be found. On the highlands the soil, timber, and general appearance of the country is different,—the soil being argillaceous and more fertile than in the lowlands, the country undulating, and much of it without timber, and covered thickly with very tall grass.

The physical geography of Africa is full of interest; but it is foreign to my object to enter upon its consideration and with this bare allusion to it I dismiss the subject.

CHAPTER II.

TOWNS—LOCALITY AND DESCRIPTION.[1]

On the banks of the rivers, and generally near a large tree, or something of the kind to mark the locality, and in villages and towns, the people all live, except that occasionally a few families collect together a short distance from the water-side, and immediately back from a town to which they are tributary.

Their towns are built without any regularity or order, having no streets or regularly laid-out walks in them. The houses being placed on the ground without method, and so close to each other that often there is barely room to pass between them, a stranger finds some difficulty in winding his way out of a large African town when he has ventured any considerable distance from the place of entrance. The great irregularity and constant windings about are well calculated to bewilder.

Some of these towns are barricaded, or fenced, in the following manner: Two rows of posts about four feet apart, planted in the earth, and extending above the ground from eight to ten feet, the posts being close to each other, make up the entire fortification. These have from two to four door-ways, which are closed at night, and often guarded during the day, if danger from war, or other cause, is apprehended.

If the reader has ever seen in the distance, and on the borders of a wood in some of our fine grazing districts, a large collection of hay-stacks, which had been some time exposed to the weather, he has in his mind a very proper image of an African town. The houses are jumbled together in a small compass. The largest town I was in, having near a thousand inhabitants, did not cover more ground than is usually occupied by a village of one hundred inhabitants in this country. In that land of wars it is unsafe to live without barricades; and hence the less ground occupied in building, the less there will be to inclose.

CHAPTER III.

HOUSES—HOW FURNISHED.

Their houses are mere mud-huts, with ground floors, wattled walls,—plastered with mud both outside and inside,—and thatched roofs. Some are square, others are circular, and hence, to make the representation referred to in the preceding chapter correct, there should be some *ricks* of grain as well as *stacks*. They have no fire-places or chimneys in their houses, though they often have fire in them during the night season, as then the ground is very damp; and the natives are fond of sleeping near the fire. The fire is placed on the ground, and the smoke is left to find its way out as best it can, generally having little difficulty, however, in making its escape, because around the eaves of the roof, if nowhere else, there is always considerable open space.

They have one or more door and window *places* in their houses, ordinarily—usually, however, without windows or doors in them; but generally they have mats suspended above the door and window places, which are dropped, like curtains, when they wish to close their houses, a thing seldom done in day-time. These houses, rude as they may seem, afford tolerable protection in a tropical climate, when they are well built. As might be inferred, they are very damp in the rainy season, and hence unhealthy to foreigners.

The best-furnished houses it was my privilege to see in that country, among real heathens, have nothing more in them than a couple of country chairs, or blocks of wood to sit upon, a couple of iron pots for cooking, a wooden bowl and a spoon or two, and a rudely-constructed bedstead, a description of which, with the bedding, will be given in another part of this book.

Immediately on the coast, and where they have mingled with white traders and missionaries, and had access to trading establishments, some of them have better furnished houses; but everywhere are houses not so well furnished as those I have described.

CHAPTER IV.

BARRAS.

In every town or village there are also from one to six barras. A barra is a mere open shed; or at best it has no more than one or two sides closed, and often none at all. In these they do their cooking, ordinarily; and from a half dozen to a dozen families use the same one for a kitchen. Some noted head-men who have many wives, have a barra to themselves, which their wives occupy not only as a kitchen, but as a workshop in general.

One or more of these in each town are called palaver-houses. These answer the same purposes which our court-houses do in this country, and are not used for the purposes alluded to above. In these palaver-houses the head-men of towns meet to adjust difficulties, settle disputes, try culprits, etc.; and when they are not thus engaged they spend much of their time in the palaver-houses playing the walle.

It was my privilege several times to be present when court was in session; and I was quite as much interested in the doings of the head-men who were officially convened to transact business, as I ever was in a court-room in America.

At one time I saw them try an adulterer. It was done in this manner: The man highest in authority occupied the *chair*. But this chair must be described: A *three-pronged limb of a tree*, with the prongs cut off,—one a little shorter than the other two, making the top incline backward,—the prongs answering for legs—being about three feet high, with a stick flattened on top, tied to the longer legs with bark, about one foot from the ground, this making the seat of the chair. On this rude chair sat the old man during the progress of the trial. All present, the chairman or judge excepted, participated in pleading the cause, some for and others against the accused. They spoke in order, one at a time, all showing due respect to the one who had the floor. The counsel, or attorneys, did not direct their remarks to the chairman particularly, but seemed to show him more deference than the others.

WOMEN IN WESTERN AFRICA.

CHAPTER V.

FOOD.

The principal article of food used by the Africans is rice; and it does not matter *what else* they have eaten, or how much, they never think they have a meal until they have swallowed at least *a pint of rice*, which, when boiled, makes *two pints!* They use, however, quite a variety of animal food, fruits, and other vegetables besides, which they eat with their rice, or between meals.

Fowls of every kind common to the country,—they have chickens in abundance, but have nothing with which to kill wild fowls—fish, which are found quite plenty in most of the rivers, rats, monkeys, frogs, alligators, ants, bugs, with whatever else the country affords, whether of the creeping, running, swimming, or flying kind, are all freely eaten.

The bug-a-bug, a species of the ant, is regarded as a great delicacy by many. Animals found dead, if not in a putrid state, are also eaten.

Their principal vegetables are rice, cocoa, potato, sweet-potato, yams, and cassada. The latter two grow in great abundance, and are highly prized as articles of food.

Their fruits are, oranges, bananas, limes, plantains, pine-apples, guavas, papaws, mangoes, African cherries, grapes, pears, sour-sops, sweet-sops, tamarinds, cocoa-nuts, and plums of various kinds. Many of these grow spontaneously, and all, as also the vegetables, are as delicious and nutritious as the fruits and vegetables of this country.

Some of the oils, especially the palm-oil, are freely used in the preparation of food, or mixed with food after cooking. In the rainy season they put a high estimate upon oil; for, as they say, the "rice stay longer and keep cold from catch them,"—meaning, that they do not become hungry so soon after eating with oil as without it, and that they do not suffer so much from cold.

CHAPTER VI.

COOKING, EATING, BATHING.

Their cooking, as to thoroughness and cleanliness,—when they are cleanly,—is not so objectionable as are some of the articles of food used.

The only cooking-utensils they have are iron pots; and ordinarily they have a large one in which to boil rice, and a smaller one in which to prepare animal food, or vegetables.

Before eating, they usually mix with the rice whatever else they may have, often turning the contents of the smaller pot into the larger, stirring all together; then taking it out into other vessels, if they have them, which seldom is the case, they give to each his portion. They eat with wooden spoons, if they have them—but this is rarely the case. They stand, or sit, or lie at their meals, as their inclination may prompt. They know nothing of the use of tables.

The more common way of eating is to gather around the pot, and convey the food from it to the mouth with the hand. They also take drink out of the hand, but sometimes they have gourds for that purpose.

Knives, forks, spoons, and water-cups are only used by those who have learned their use from traders or missionaries.

They eat but twice a day, and generally between nine and ten o'clock A. M. and five and six o'clock P. M.

They are the most gluttonous eaters I have ever seen or heard of; and to offset this, they can go an unusually long time without food, and still perform ordinary labor.

I have known workmen in the employ of the mission to refuse their ration of rice—which is a quart per day—and labor all day without tasting food, *for the pleasure of having what they call a good full, or two quarts to eat the next day!*

Boatmen will eat one and a half quarts at one meal, which is three quarts when boiled. It affords an African no little pleasure to eat his fill. An old head-man who had ten wives laughed most heartily at me once on seeing me leave a plate of rice, after eating about one fourth of it. He then turned to the company, and said, "White man eat but *little, little* (mincing with his mouth as he spoke); and no wonder he can have but one wife, and must soon die in black man's country; but black man he can eat plenty, and full himself good fashion, and then he can be strong, and have plenty wife. He no go die soon like white man."

After eating they generally wash their mouths, both outside and in, and sometimes *their whole faces*, if within the reach of water.

They have no regular time for bathing, but often do it early in the morning or late at night.

CHAPTER VII.

DRESS.

The dress of the African is little better than none, if we except that worn by some of the headmen of towns. The aristocracy and "big gentlemen pass everybody else," whose dress is hardly passable for even a warm country.

The Mohammedans commonly wear the Mandingo shirt, which is a loose gown with flowing sleeves. It makes not only a decent, but a comfortable covering for the body in a tropical climate, and is decidedly superior to the best clothes used by the other natives. With them, a country cloth tied around the waist often forms the only article of clothing worn by both sexes. Many of both sexes have nothing on their persons but a totranger, and young females sometimes have nothing but a girdle of beads fastened around the waist. And worse than all, many of the young people—sometimes old ones—are in a state of entire nudity.

Children taken into the mission-schools feel

ashamed when clothing is put upon them, and not unfrequently are they persecuted by their friends for "turning white people." When any dress like white people, or adopt the customs and fashions of the whites, others say, "*they done turn white man.*"

Children at the schools, if not watched, will throw off their clothing; and when alone they love to do this, and have a good romp, then put them on again—and with them a long, sober face,—before coming into the presence of the missionary or teacher again.

Many of them, young and old, seem to have a natural dislike to clothing; for even head-men when visited unawares, are sometimes found naked.

The warmth of the climate accounts for this, in part; for certainly the biting frosts of December in this country would not only change their tastes in this particular, but would cause them to put forth effectual efforts to procure clothing. "Necessity is the mother of invention," and a father to provide.

CHAPTER VIII.

THEIR SLEEPING-FIXTURES.

Nearly every African hut has a rudely-constructed bedstead, only wide enough for one person to lie in, and is made in the following manner: Four poles placed on end constitute the posts; poles tied to them with bark make the rails, and other poles placed on them support the bedding. Branches of trees, or grass, make the mattress, upon which are placed two country cloths, one for an under and the other for the upper covering; and this makes the best beds we saw among the real heathen. In this bed the *man of the house* generally sleeps, while his wives, children, and slaves sleep on the ground, with only a grass-mat, or country cloth, between them and mother earth, the covering being also a country cloth, if there be any at all!

Some houses are furnished with from one to two hammocks, in which some of the household sleep, swinging above *terra firma*.

Ordinarily they have fire in their houses during the night; and those sleeping on the ground lie with their heads next to the fire. If they have covering at all, they always cover the face, wrapping in the whole head closely, while the legs and feet turned from the fire are naked. Whether awake or asleep, they prefer that the head should be hottest; and we have seen them sleeping in daytime with their legs in the shade, head in the sun, and a stone for a pillow, while a vertical sun was pouring his rays down upon them with the fierce intensity of the tropics. It may be best that their sleeping accommodations are no better; for as they are, they sleep too much. An African can sleep sixteen hours out of the twenty-four and feel none the worse for it. There are, however, some exceptions to this rule, especially among those who have become civilized,—some of whom are wide awake sixteen hours out of twenty-four, and make it necessary for those living among them to keep their eyes open and watch, as well as pray, lest they enter into temptation and sustain loss.

CHAPTER IX.

LABOR, FARMING, MANUFACTURES, TRADES.

They have no regular business or employment; and especially is this true of the men; for, *as a rule*, they never labor unless driven to it by *necessity*. There is, indeed, little inducement to labor in the present state of society. The natural productions of the country are so abundant, and the wants of the people—in their estimation—so few, that there is nothing to excite to industry and enterprise.

If they have no clothing they go without. If they are without rice they draw from nature, both from water and land, often subsisting on that which is scarcely fit for animals to eat. If they have no shelter in which to lodge they do without, as in the case of clothing. The climate being warm, and their houses as a general thing not being proof against dampness, they suffer no *great* inconvenience to be without them a large part of the year, especially during the dry season.

The country being held in common by the chiefs, who are also head-men of towns, there is no such thing as property in real estate; and if one a little more industrious than his fellows does labor and economize until he stores up a quantity of rice, or anything else in the way of persona property, head-men will extort from him, and others sponge upon him, until the fruits of his labor are gone. If one had it in his heart to lay up for a time of need, or for his progeny, he would not be able to do so.

What farming they do is very imperfectly done, and on a small scale. Having no horses or oxen, or animals of any kind, with which to cultivate the soil, and being entirely without farming utensils, save a rudely-constructed hoe, they can not cultivate the soil to advantage. With the hoe they loosen up the surface of the ground a little, and cultivate rice, cassada, cocoa, potatoes, sweet-potatoes, yams, etc. Rice and cassada are the staple commodities of agriculture.

The women do most of the farming, as well as every other kind of work, with the exception that the men generally clear off the ground. This they do with the ax and cutlass. An African ax is some longer, but not much more than half as broad as ours. It is a poor affair to chop with. But they only chop off the trees and bush, and then let them lie during one dry season, or until they become so dry that they burn up without further trouble, when fire is put to them.

Their superficial method of agriculture, as a matter of course, soon exhausts the soil. Seldom is the same spot cultivated more than two or three years until it is left, and before it becomes sufficiently replenished to be productive again it is overgrown with bush and saplings of considerable size. There being no winter, shrubbery grows rapidly; and it is astonishing to one who has lived in a cold latitude to see the height to which it attains in a single year. From one to five acres is as much as a family cultivates at the same time, but from two to three crops may be grown the same year.

They also manufacture palm-oil, which is made from the shuck or hull of the nut; and a very superior oil is made of the kernel of the palm-nut, which is called nut-oil. This is quite as good for culinary purposes as lard, and makes a very superior burning-fluid.

Country cloths are made by them from cotton, which grows spontaneously. Cotton grows on bushes about the size of the currant-bush, and some on what is called the cotton-tree, which is the largest of the forest. Some of these trees measure ten feet and more in diameter at their base.

The manner of spinning is somewhat ingenious A spindle fastened to a long stick, put in motion with the fingers like a top, makes the entire spinning machinery.

The thread thus made is woven in strips of from four to six inches wide, and these are sewed together until the size desired is obtained. The thread, though coarse, is tolerably even, and the weaving is also passably good.

Most of these cloths are colored, and the figures of some are very tastefully executed. The indigo-plant is a native of the country and is much used in coloring. These cloths make excellent bed-spreads, table-spreads, piano-covers, etc., in this country. They also manufacture grass-mats in great abundance, and some of excellent quality. These they make by hand altogether, as they do their country cloths. Mats are also made of the bamboo branch.

Blys, or baskets, are made from the ratan twig, which is very flexible, and not easily broken, and hence is well adapted to that purpose.

The only trades, or approximation to trades, they have, are canoe-building and blacksmithing —of the latter only enough to make iron-fastenings for canoes, and a few rude implements of husbandry and of war. The canoe made from the tree is raised by fastening timbers on its sides, and then boarding up. In this way, and by spreading them a little, they make them sufficiently large to bear from six to ten tons burden. Their only modes of transportation are by canoes on the rivers, and by portage overland. Neither have they any traveling facilities, but by canoes on the water and afoot on the land.

The reason I say they have no other trades but the two referred to above, is simply because all seem to understand how to do whatever else is done—even to house-building—without serving an apprenticeship.

I once asked a conoe-builder if the boy assisting him at the time was his son. "No," he replied, "I only take him to learn him canoe-sense." He meant, of course, the trade of canoe-building.

CHAPTER X.

WAR.

Much of the time of the men is still taken up in the prosecution of wars. They often engage in wars as neighbors in this country gather in their harvests; namely, one tribe assists another. The headman of the town will furnish so many men for another head-man with whom he is friendly, to enable the latter to do the work of destruction upon an enemy.

These persons must be fed, during the time of their service, from the stores of the tribe or headmen whom they serve. While at Shengay during the first three months of the year 1875, a war party came close there several times, so that the people of the town at different times brought their goods, and came themselves to the mission-house for protection.

There was also war on the Big Boom and Bargru rivers during my stay in Africa. White people should take to themselves much blame for this state of things, as I shall presently show.

CHAPTER XI.

AMUSEMENTS.

There is quite a variety of amusements among them; and no small part of their time is thus spent, especially by the men in time of peace. They practice various dances. One is called the "country dance," another the "devil's dance." By the way, would not the latter be an appropriate name for most all dancing, as it is now practiced, both in enlightened and in heathen countries? They have their country drums and fiddles,—and strange-looking things they are,—to make music on such occasions. As in America, the whole night is sometimes spent in dancing, and both sexes participate in the amusement.

Playing the walle is a more common amusement, especially among head-men, and others of note. Walle is often played for gain, but whether it is a game of chance, or purely of sleight, I was not able to discover.

This much I know, that bits of tobacco about

AFRICAN FIDDLE AND WALLE BOWL.

AFRICAN GODDESS.

AFRICAN AX AND HOE.

the size of a man's hand (the tobacco in that country is used in the leaf as it grows), or a few needles or spoons, or whatever else may be on hand as an article of commerce," is staked and played for. When they have nothing to stake they play for amusement only.

Walles are public property, sometimes furnished at the expense of the town, each town having one or more of them. Ordinarily they are kept in the palaver-house, where there are also hammocks swung to accommodate loungers.

Between playing the walle, and sleeping in the hammocks, head-men while away their leisure hours, while their wives are close by in groups, making mats, spinning cotton, preparing the meal, or else in the field planting and looking after the the crops, which are mostly cassada and rice.

Women do all the drudgery and hard work in Africa, and many of them are compelled to labor hard to procure a livelihood for themselves, children, and husbands. With an infant lashed fast to her back, the mother may be seen in the field hoeing, pulling weeds, gathering in the crop of rice, carrying fire-wood from the forest, or in the river washing clothes. Of the latter they have little to do, however. The way of washing is worthy of notice. This they do by going into the water's edge, dipping the clothes into the water.

and then beating them upon a rock, or log, which is placed there for the purpose.

Our hearts sadden when we contemplate the condition of the heathen female. No sight was more revolting to my feelings in that country, than to see an infant tied fast to the back of its mother, swinging back and forth, with a vertical sun darting his rays full in its face, without even the covering of a bonnet or anything of the kind to shield it from the heat, while the mother, with every stroke of her hoe, or the cloth she was throwing upon the rock to beat the dirt out of it, added pain to her child.

CHAPTER XII.

THEIR PHYSICAL STRUCTURE.

The physiognomical and physiological structure of the people with whom I became acquainted in Africa is better than that of the colored race in this country. Especially is this true of their physiognomy. The flat nose and thick lip are not so common as among that race of people in this country; and on the other hand, the prominent forehead, the expressive eye, and the intelligent countenance are as frequently seen as in *any country it has been my privilege to visit.*

They have well-developed chests, and the most erect carriage of any people of my knowledge. This is especially to be remarked of the Mohammedans, of whom it may be said with emphasis that their dignified and independent walk, and their lordly appearance in whatever position they may occupy, with a self-righteousness and self-esteem as prominent as their depravity is deep, make them to fill up the character of a Pharisee, as described by the Savior in the New Testament.

They are decidedly a superior race of people,—much more intelligent and enterprising than the heathen proper, though no less sunken in vice. We shall say more of them in another part of this work.

It is true that the general appearance of the most stupid Africans indicates susceptibility of mental culture; and from actual experiment, by different missionaries, the evidence is conclusive on this point. Their children between the ages of five and fifteen years are, all things considered, quite as susceptible of intellectual improvement as are the white children of this country. In the study of those branches of science requiring the exercise of memory, mainly, such as geography and history, they fully compete with American children; but in the study of those branches of science which require the exercise of the reasoning faculties, they are inferior to the children of this country.

It requires no supernatural ken, however, to discover the reason for this. Rather should we wonder that these people have powers of intellect at all, after suffering as they have for centuries the blasting and deteriorating influences of heathenism, and the tyrannical and hellish treatment they have received from slave-traders, and others who have gone among them, and are among them now, for worldy gain alone. Surely, on African soil, "man's inhumanity to man" has caused not only millions to mourn, but very many to sink to depths in the pool of moral pollution to which they never would have gone had they been left to themselves.

It is but proper to state also, in this connection, that their skill in chirography is equalled by few, and not surpassed by any. They are naturally great imitators in whatever direction they choose to exercise their faculties. They are remarkably skillful with the pen.

CHAPTER XIII.

DISPOSITIONS—TASTE FOR MUSIC.

I do not think the Africans are naturally ill-natured; but on the contrary, they are remarkable for their good nature and pleasant manners to strangers. Indeed, one great obstacle in the way of their Christianization is the fact that they are not sufficiently excitable. I hope I am not misunderstood.

They are fond of every kind of music, and sing a great deal, whether at work or play. When rowing me along the river and plying their oars with all their strength, they would sing at least half of the time, unless they had a particular cause for not doing so.

When our boatmen or workmen omitted singing, we took it for granted that they were vexed or sick. There as here, people seldom sing when in a bad humor. The common way with boatmen is for one to lead the singing, making the music as he proceeds, all but the chorus, in which all the party join, making perfect harmony—of their kind; and tossing their heads triumphantly, with mouths wide open, the contrast between the color of their skin and teeth challenges the attention of the most indifferent.

The principal part of the music is sung alternately with the chorus; and when all join in the chorus a new impetus is given to the canoe. It is scarcely necessary to say that they have musical voices, strong lungs, and that they have not yet learned to primp their mouths and mew—like many of the people of this country, especially America's last edition,—when they sing.

As might be expected, they are vain and fond of praise. A little praise elates them much; and if the praiser should ever after reprove, he is at once reminded of his former flattering opinion.

CHAPTER XIV.

DECEPTIONS.

There is no end to their deceptions on foreigners; and often their pretenses have so much show of reality that the most discriminating are shamefully humbugged. Sometimes their plans are laid far ahead, and with so much skill, tact, and cunning that one must be wide awake to keep out of their meshes. When they set themselves for guileful ends they never draw back until they succeed, unless absolutely compelled to do so.

They cheat in the sale of nearly every article they sell to white persons, if not closely watched; and the only restraint they seem to feel in the matter arises from the fear of detection and punishment.

An old sea-captain, who had been spending his winters on the south and west coasts of Africa for many years, told me he had known them to manufacture a mixture of clay, water, and oil which much resembled the palm-oil, and sell fothe *pure oil* that which was three-fourth parts clay and water. He has also known them, with true Yankee ingenuity, to hollow out balls of bees-wax and fill the vacuum with sand, closing the sand in so neatly as to avoid detection.

They also take the juice of camwood and stain other wood with it, making such a perfect imitation that no one suspects the deception. They have been known too to manufacture an ingenious imitation of ivory, and sell it to traders for the pure article. They adulterate gold, and palm off the spurious article upon the trader.

I have been too often defeated while they were in my employ as oarsmen to believe anything else than that they possess, naturally, as much mind as their paler brethren. It is their custom to stop at almost every village and town on the river when they travel with canoes; and in order to make better speed, I would, by stratagem and the exercise of dictatorial power, do my utmost to prevent this. Often my attempts were vain.

If persuasion, or the promise to pull the harder to make up the loss of time, or some other plea, would not induce me to let them stop, before I got to the next town the fire would be out, or the spile out of the water-cask, or something else would occur that made it absolutely necessary to land. Never shall I forget the fattening laugh which my men took over my defeat, as they pulled up the canoe to a certain town to get water. Only two hours before we had at least ten gallons, but in the nick of time all was gone. The oarsman sitting next to me, and not over four feet from me, managed to ply his toes on the spile of the water-cask while handling the oar, and thus let the water out.

Let those who deny them a rational soul, and go so far as to call them brainless resemblances of the human species, tell us why other animals do not exhibit such skill and forethought in carrying out their purposes. They exercise so much ingenuity, calculation, and reason in all they undertake,—mainly for wicked ends, I admit,—that no unprejudiced and sincere mind can doubt their rationality.

They have the elements in their nature to make them an inventive, enterprising, and prosperous people; but, as in the uncultivated field, weeds only are produced. Not until the plow of gospel truth destroys the weeds of sin and prepares the soil for the reception of the seed of God's word can we hope for a bountiful crop of souls, purified and saved.

CHAPTER XV.

EVANGELIZATION—ITS DIFFICULTIES.

The greatest discouragement the missionary has to contend with in laboring among that people, is the fact that he can not give them a clear apprehension of spiritual truth when first going among them, or when commencing at a new point.

For want of a proper medium by which to convey ideas, he fails, to a great extent, to place the truths of salvation before them in an intelligent form. To get figures which they understand by which to illustrate gospel truth, and bring it to bear upon their hearts and consciences, so as to produce conviction of sin, and a desire to be freed from it, is difficult.

Their habits of life and modes of thinking differ so widely from ours that the most simple and easily understood illustrations used by us are misunderstood, or fail to convey any meaning at all. After making the truth as simple and plain as it can be made, by the use of the most simple language, we yet fail to give them clear conceptions of it.

It is highly important that the missionary learn their language, become familiar with their usages, manner of life, views of propriety, and their secret abominations, in order that he may labor among them successfully.

On a certain occasion I preached from the parable of the vine and branches, in the 15th chapter of the Gospel according to John. I showed that as the branches are in the vine so we must be in Christ; that the Christian is as dependent upon Christ for spiritual life as the branches are on the vine, and as intimately related to him as the branch is to the vine. I endeavored to explain how we might become branches of the "true vine," and thus be saved from sin and hell.

Though I was as plain as I could be, yet the whole sermon was lost, because, as I afterward learned, none of my hearers—not even my interpreter—knew what the word "*vine*" meant! They call vines "country ropes." I refer to this to give the reader an idea of the difficulty of preaching intelligently to that people without a knowledge of their language.

But that which should be done *can* be done; and if we resolve in God's name that what should and can be done in the way of evangelizing the inhabitants of Africa SHALL be done, it will not be long until that people will have the gospel preached to them understandingly.

All, it is presumed, will agree with me that they should have a pure gospel preached to them; and if the adage referred to be truthful, it *can* be done. It only remains for Christians to say when it shall be accomplished. God has declared by revelation that it SHALL be done. (Matt. xxiv. 14.) Will we act our part in the accomplishment of this great and glorious work, and thus be co-workers with him in winning this world back to Christ?

CHAPTER XVI.

LANGUAGES.

The languages and dialects of the people are very defective in words, and especially in words by which to express abstract ideas. Hence they fail to give definite ideas of quantity, quality, time, distance, number, and so on; and in the absence of any written language, or standard of language, a mongrel speech of English, French, and Spanish, with various native dialects, has obtained, which is better calculated to excite laughter, often, than to communicate thought. To give a description of quantity they say, "not much," or "little much," or "plenty much," and of quality, they say, "good a little," or "good too much;" of distance, "not far," "far a little," or "far too much;" and by the way of the river they say, "so many points,"—meaning the bends in the river,—and the traveler is left to find out as he goes along whether these bends are the fourth of a mile, or four miles apart.

Sometimes in giving the distance from one place to another, they say, "if you start when sun comes up, you catch when he stand so," pointing to the sky where they suppose the sun will be when the traveler arrives at the place, if the journey be made in the common time. These examples furnish a pretty fair illustration of how clearly and definitely they express ideas, as a general thing; but some of their forms of speech are remarkable for their pertinence and significance.

If they wish to tell you that a person is ignorant,—for in that country, as here, they have their higher and lower classes, their aristocracy and common people,—they say, "no light broke upon him yet." If they wish to tell you that a judgment has been sent upon a town, they say that town—telling where the place is—"catch one God flog." Though these forms of speech are awkward, yet who can more clearly convey the ideas with the same number of words?

The English will doubtless eventually be the prevailing language among the tribes on the west coast.

CHAPTER XVII.

MARKING TIME, COUNTING, ETC.

Their only way of marking time is, by the moon and the seasons of the year. To tell how long since an event transpired, they say, "so many moons," or "so many rainy seasons," have elapsed. They know of no division of time into weeks, hours, and minutes. They have no knowledge of a Sabbath, or day of rest. If the theory of some, however, be correct, namely, that we do not require the seventh part of our time in which to rest, unless we work too hard the six days appointed by God in which to labor, THEY do not need a Sabbath. But away with such infidelity.

One day as I visited a town some ten miles distant from Good Hope Station I was forcibly impressed with the fact that the influence of that mission was being felt in establishing the sacredness of the holy Sabbath even there. The headman of the town remarked that he was going to bring us cocoa-nuts to sell to-morrow; but turn-

CHIEF CAULKER'S RESIDENCE AND THE BARRA IN SHENGAY.

ing and looking upon the wall of his hut just after saying this, he continued, "No, not to-morrow, for that is Sunday-day, and mission no trade on that day."

Upon casting my eyes around I saw a flat piece of wood with seven holes in it, hanging on the wall, and a peg in the lowest. The topmost hole in his almanac was Sunday, and by moving the peg every day he knew when it came. Whether he had ever been at the mission-station I do not know, but from some source he had learned that missionaries kept one day out of seven sacred, and that it would be useless to bring cocoa-nuts to sell on that day.

Many of the Sherbro people can count no higher than ten, and can not do that without splicing words together, thus: "Bull—one, Ting—two, Errah—three, Heall—four, Maan—five." Then they take one and put it to five to make six, thus: "Maan-bull—six, Maan-ting—seven, Maan-errah—eight, Maan-heall—nine, and Wang—ten." Here the counting process stops with many of the Sherbros; but the Mendi and Timiny tribes can count higher, even to hundreds.

They are assisted very much in communicating ideas by the great variety of *gestures* which they use in conversation. Their gestures are very appropriate and significant, and by no means con-

4

fined to the use of the hands alone. When an African talks he talks all over—with head, eyes, face, arms, and legs. They use their feet and legs as freely, when necessary, as any other member of the body. I have seen them stoop forward with the face half way to the ground, then again bend back as far as they could, and throw their bodies from side to side, to assist in the utterance of their thoughts.

They are also assisted in this by the use of numerous EMBLEMS, PARABLES, SYMBOLS, IMAGES, ETC. These assist them much in showing the relation of one thing to another, and the estimate they put upon things and persons.

For instance, if a head-man wishes to make an expression of good-will and friendship to another head-man, he simply sends him a piece of white cloth. If a bride wishes to let everybody know that she is married, she ties a white string around her forehead. If a man wishes to farm a piece of land which is yet in timber, he puts on its boundaries sticks with leaves tied to their tops. If a head-man wishes to announce that persons will be punished for throwing water where he does not wish it in his town, he puts up a stake in the place with a bunch of switches tied to its top.

While I was at Good Hope Station, Mr. Brooks received from a head-man, whom he had once visited, a present of a goat, a piece of soap, and six country cloths. The goat, soap, and each one of the cloths were emblematical of some specific thing, which the messenger who brought them explained to Mr. B. at the time. A great variety of things are thus represented, and this assists them not a little to make plain what their defective language alone would fail to do.

CHAPTER XVIII.

ETIQUETTE.

A good deal of etiquette is observed among them, which, as might be supposed, is modeled after their own peculiar ideas. On special occasions, in particular places, and toward particular persons, certain ceremonies *must always be observed*.

For instance, to go into a town and not call upon the head-man of the place immediately, is treating him impolitely. The proper way is to call upon the head-man at once, and tell him whence you are and whither you are bound, and whether you are going to proceed immediately on the journey, or stay with him to "to cook," or for the night.

If a night's lodging is wanted, the stranger must "shake the king's hand;" that is, make him a present to the value of the things and privileges required. In this case a house is furnished for the exclusive accommodation of the traveler and his men, and will not be used by any others during his stay in town. If a person stays more than one night, it is expected that he call upon the head-man of the town each morning, and say "How you do" to him. On leaving the place the traveler must pay his parting respects to his landlord. By observing these customs, head-men feel responsible for the safety of the traveler and his goods to some extent, and will often befriend him.

To refuse a present, no difference of how little value, is treating the one offering it impolitely, and is considered sufficient ground for palaver. Persons of note treat head-men impolitely if they pass their towns without stopping and paying them their respects. It is regarded as a token of respect to call on persons at any time, to say "How do you do" to them.

We were much amused one Sabbath morning, just at the hour of worship, and while we were reading the Scriptures, to see one of the workmen in the employ of the mission come to the door and beckon with his hand to a brother missionary who had charge of that station, and who was seated on the other side of the room, to come to him. He went to the door, and asked him what he wanted. He replied: "Oh, me only come for say how do you do; no more."

Their meeting and parting salutations are strictly observed. I was taken to task several times by head-men for leaving them without observing the Ippeoway and Mogmdawa—parting salutation. When very great friends meet they rub each other's arms with the hand several times, and afterward shake hands a long time.

There is quite as much etiquette among them as there is among us, but it is of a different kind; and by the observance of their rules, so far as it can be done in conscience, one may get along with and among them very well. They are not a dangerous people to dwell among if proper care be taken.

They will beg and cheat one out of all he has if they can, and if a good opportunity serves for escape they will steal his goods; but there is no danger of being robbed, or injured in person, if proper precaution be taken. Some of them are strictly honest, however; but this is the exception, and not the rule.

CHAPTER XIX.

ANCIENT CUSTOMS.

They observe many ancient customs. For example: They take the finest flour, best rice, purest oil, and the best of whatever they use as food themselves, prepare them in the best style, and offer them in sacrifice to their deities. Those familiar with the Old Testament know that the Jews were required to take the best of their flocks and sacrifice to the Lord. Some of them also wear sandals, as the people did anciently.

They sometimes wash the feet of strangers coming to them, which is also an ancient custom. If the traveler be a common person, the head-man's slaves or wives wash his feet; but if he be a man of note, the head-man washes them himself, to show the respect in which he holds him. Washing feet is a custom founded upon a physical necessity in warm countries, as much as wearing clothes is in cold countries; and when spoken of in the Scriptures as a religious act, it means nothing more than administering to others' wants, and is a duty similar to that of clothing the naked or feeding the hungry.

In warm, dusty countries, where the people seldom have clothes upon the legs below the knees, and at best nothing but sandals on their feet, washing the feet often, and especially after traveling, is conducive to both health and comfort. Washing feet in cold water also quenches thirst, and washing the whole body does it more effectually. I tested this several times when unable to quench my thirst by drinking alone.

Their method of expressing grief and sorrow is ancient. When in great grief, or trouble, they put on the coarsest clothes they have, throw ashes and dirt upon themselves, dishevel their hair, and smite upon their breasts. When mourning for the dead with their mourning habiliments upon them, and their hair on end, wringing their hands and smiting upon their breasts, they look like a bundle of misery most ungracefully put together —whether so in *heart*, does not always appear

CHAPTER XX.

LAWS, GOVERNMENT.

It may be said that they have laws. They have no written laws, however, but rules and regulations, handed down by tradition from one generation to another.

There are, first, what may be termed *general laws*, which extend to people of different towns. The chiefs and head-men of a certain region of country embracing a number of towns meet together and agree upon a code of laws by which to regulate the people in their intercourse with each other, especially for purposes of trade and commerce. All the people of the district represented are required to keep these laws; and if the head-man or the people of any town violate them, those of the other towns have just cause for palaver with the offending party; and as a general thing they require so much produce, or goods, as an indemnity, "to cool their hearts," as they say.

If the offending town refuses to pay, or to make satisfaction to the others, they make war upon it, and if victorious, sell the prisoners for slaves. The most trifling breach of law is sometimes made a cause for war upon a *weak* town for the sake of the profits accruing from the sale of the prisoners. The Africans, like enlightened people, prefer to make war upon the *weak*.

Head-men also enact such *laws* as they think necessary for the government of their own people. These they repeal or alter as circumstances seem to require, or so as to bring the greatest revenue into their own coffers. Many of their laws bear the impress of injustice and cruelty, and are made with a view of extorting money, or its equivalent, from the common people.

At Mo-Colong, when war was in progress there a few years since, a law was passed that no one should carry a whole bunch of bananas or plantains into the town at once. If any attempted to do so, others had a right to take all from the owner and divide it among themselves. The scarcity of provisions was the alleged reason for the passage of such a law.

There is also what might be called the higher or supreme law, which is made by a *secret society* called Purrow, or Devil-Bush Society. Laws made by this society, coming in collision with the common law of the town, have the pre-eminence. We shall give a separate chapter on the doings of the Purrow-bush society.

From the above the reader may infer the form of government that exists. It is not a monarchy, but an approximation to that form of government. Not unfrequently is the country given up to anarchy and confusion, and is kept in that condition, much of the time, by those pretended rulers whose only aim is to get possession of the earnings of the people, and waste them upon their own lusts.

CHAPTER XXI

OATHS, CURRENCY.

They have a method of administering oaths, by which to secure a statement of facts from those giving testimony. Upon this point, however, I can not give much definite information.

I was told by a native of that country that some tribes swore upon salt, and others upon snuff. So far as I was able to learn, each tribe swears by what it considers the most sacred thing; and ordinarily they have a great regard for their oaths.

Every article of exchange in that country is called money, and besides this they have no currency at all. The best currency there are rum and tobacco; and next to these may be named prints, cotton goods, fish-hooks, iron spoons, small mirrors, needles, and iron pots. The English make a goods called blue baft, which is in great demand. Hoes, axes, and such things as they can use, may also be exchanged for their produce, at a good profit. Owing to the fact that they have no standard of money, articles of exchange often have no regular price or value attached to them. This gives traders a great chance for extortion, which they not unfrequently improve, to the injury of the poor, ignorant people among whom they transact business.

The influence of this class of men from civilized countries is, as a rule, most detrimental to the work of missions. They are generally wicked themselves; and then they deal largely in rum and tobacco, and other hurtful things. Rum in Africa, as in other countries, leads to almost all manner of crime. But more of this in another part of this work.

CHAPTER XXII.

MATRIMONY, ABUSE OF WOMEN.

I now come to speak of a subject which, though not pleasant, goes far to show the deep degradation of that people. I mean their customs regulating the marriage relation, and the conduct of the men toward the women.

Every man almost has his wife, or wives, and ordinarily each has as many as he can afford to buy. Wives are bought there as animals are in this country. Usually they are not consulted in the choice of their husbands at all, but are compelled to be the partners of whoever happens to furnish their parents the amount of goods asked for them.

Wives are often not allowed to eat with their husbands, nor walk by their sides, but must walk behind them to show that they are in subjection. They are also often severely flogged by them, for, in their own language, "they no be good wife till she get one flog." I often saw the cruel welts of the flogging process on the backs of women; and one woman came to Good Hope to seek protection from her cruel husband. She had been tied to the ground, in which position her tongue was drawn out of her mouth and burned with a red-hot iron!

Though women are called wives, they are in reality slaves, having no *rights*, and only such *privileges* as hard-hearted, superstitious, ignorant heathen husbands are disposed to give them. And it matters not how cruelly they may be treated, it is seldom that their wrongs are redressed; because there is no appeal from the decisions of their husbands except in rare and extraordinary cases, when head-men are induced to put bounds to the wrongs imposed upon them by their tyrannical masters.

As a general thing the wife must raise the husband's rice, prepare his food, row his canoe along the river, do all his drudgery, and take such flogging in the bargain as he is disposed to give her.

A man wishing a wife goes to the *parents* of the one selected, and makes them a present of a country cloth, a few mats, or some article of the kind, at the same time making known his request. The man's wealth, or ability to give, regulates the value of the present he makes, commonly ranging in value from one half to two dollars.

The parents and family put the applicant off at first, and generally keep him in suspense as long as there is hope of getting more money for the girl. If the man is intent on having her he continues to call on her parents, carrying a present each time. To go without one would destroy his prospects altogether. Thus they keep the applicant coming until they think they have obtained all there is a possibility of getting for the daughter, and then he is told he can have her. No marriage ceremony is performed. When the price is paid the bride is taken away, if the husband so desires.

After men have one wife they sometimes continue to work until they have means to purchase the second, and then they cease to work altogether or do but little. Two wives are considered a competency, or a livelihood. It is thought two women ought to be able to support one man; and hence those who have them may retire from active business and live upon their earnings.

A man's wealth and authority is estimated by the number of his wives. He who has twenty, has twice the wealth and authority of the one who has but ten.

Wives are property to all intents and purposes; and though it is disreputable for a man to sell his wife, yet they often manage to get rid of them, if a sufficient compensation is offered. They have little conscience in the matter. Sometimes they manage to prove an accusation against them, which they make an excuse for selling them into slavery, or to dispose of them in other ways.

Marriage contracts are often made for girls when they are not more than five or six years old. In this case the betrothment money, or most of it, is not paid until near the time of marriage,—that is when the girl is thirteen or fourteen years old. It is considered a reproach for girls to pass twelve years of age without having an offer for marriage. Indeed they are frequently married at that age.

While I was at Good Hope Station a man came there making inquiry for his wife. Seeing the girls in the room he went to one about six years of age, laid his hand upon her head, and said to me, "This one my wife; my father done buy her for me long time ago." He was soon made acquainted with the fact that he could not have her then nor at any subsequent period, with the consent of the missionaries.

The children taken at that station were given to the missionaries to be kept until they should arrive at their majority, with the condition that they should then be their own masters,—neither the parents nor the missionaries having further control over them.

Parents are willing to give up their children

thus, and give book—a written agreement—to that effect. This is a very proper way, in the opinion of many missionaries, to take children to instruct in the truths of Christianity; for if taken young, and if proper training be given, by the time they are of age they become so well established in the principles of Christian morality that they are likely to adhere to them through life.

Daughters are emphatically the readiest cash article parents have for sale, and those who have a number easily get a livelihood. Parents rejoice when daughters are born to them, and say, "That good too much." The reason is obvious.

Another fruitful source of wife-getting arises from the decease of wealthy head-men. Soon after one dies, the male members of his family—relatives—meet together to make a distribution of his goods and property, and his wives, in common with other property, are distributed among the heirs to the estate, and become the wives of the legatees. If any refuse to go with those to whom they fall by inheritance, they are put into a dark mud-hut, and left without food or drink, or punished in some other way, until they acquiesce in the arrangement.

Men continue to get wives as long as they have means, without reference to age, or the number they already have. Kissicummah, a Mohammedan chief, who was very old and frail, was still getting wives. When visiting in his town I asked his son how many wives his father had. He replied, "I know not; but he have plenty, for he commence getting wife when he was first man, and he keep getting wife yet, for there one he get last week," pointing to a girl of about fourteen or fifteen years of age.

And now, ladies and mothers of America, why are you in a happier condition than your sex in Africa? Why are your rights respected, and your position in society made honorable? Why are you not oppressed and brutalized, as women are in Africa? Why are you not bought and sold, and cruelly flogged and mistreated generally? Simply *because the Bible of God is among you.* Where that book is not, women suffer cruel injustice.

But we would also ask, What would you take to exchange your happy condition with the one of those spoken of in this chapter? What would you take, mothers, to have your daughters in the condition of young women in Africa, exposed to the hellish cruelties, and the soul and body polluting influences of heathenism? Aside from the refining influences of Christianity, neither you, your children, nor your husbands possess any more moral excellence or regard for the happiness and rights of others than do the oppressed people of the land of Ham.

We are indebted to the Bible for all the intelligence, enterprise, and refinement we have above the heathen; and take from us the Bible and its influences, and in a very few centuries our condition would in every respect be as wretched as that of the most degraded race on the face of the globe. Mankind, the world over, are much alike when left to the degrading tendencies of their corrupt natures; for "they are all gone aside, they are all together become filthy: there is none that doeth good, no, not one." "They profess that they know God; but in works they deny him, being abominable, disobedient, and to every good work reprobate."

Could Christian women in this land, and all Christians, realize how much they are indebted to the gospel for the unnumbered and exceeding high privileges they enjoy, surely they would make greater efforts to give the bread of life to the thousands who are perishing.

Should we not all be missionaries, in sympathy, feeling, action? And should not the burdening inquiry of our life be, "How can I best promote this great work?"

If the consolations and hopes of religion are to us of more value than all the world, will we not have others enjoy them? Did not the first emotions of our souls at conversion fill us with a longing for the salvation of others? Did we not feel then that we could endure any privation, make any sacrifice, and perform any labor possible to save others? Does not the Spirit of Christ always fill the soul with yearnings for the salvation of others, and impart to those who possess it a desire to consecrate themselves fully to the work of the world's evangelization?

CHAPTER XXIII.

FUNERAL CEREMONIES, WITCHCRAFT.

There are many things connected with their funeral ceremonies and notions of death which are both foolish and wicked.

Often as soon as persons die they are opened, to ascertain whether witches killed them or not. If the liver is enlarged, or any of the internal organs have an unnatural appearance,—a very common thing in that malarious country,—they say "witch killed them." Indeed if what I saw be a correct criterion by which to judge of the matter, nearly all the deaths that occur are the work of witches, either directly or indirectly.

At York Island, a town in which I preached several times, a youth was killed by an alligator while bathing in the river. The people said, "Some witch turned alligator and killed him." Subsequently a man was killed near Kaw Mendi Station, by a leopard, and the people there said, "Some witch turned leopard and killed him." Very many things are ascribed to the work of witches— such as sudden turns in fortune, diseases of different kinds, and extraordinary incidents in life.

When anything occurs which is supposed to be the work of witches, no matter what it is, some person or persons are apprehended as the guilty party; and the "witch-master's" skill,—or more correctly expressed, his deception, trickery, and groundless assumption,—becomes the umpire to establish the innocence or guilt of the accused.

Another mode of trial is to give the accused poisonous drinks, which they say are fatal if the person is guilty, but harmless if innocent. If the victim be an enemy of those trying him, death is certain; but if a friend, they may easily save his life by making the poisonous draught very weak.

The draught generally administered is a decoction of the sassy-wood bark, and when strong is a rank poison; but if too large a draught is given it acts as an emetic, and in this case death does not result.

When persons have been convicted of witchcraft they are tortured in various ways, mostly until death ends their sufferings. They are tortured first to ascertain whether they are guilty, and then if convicted for the supposed crime, they are punished most cruelly

At the town of Manyua, then an out-station of

Mendi Mission, a man was accused of witchcraft, and given the sassy-bark tea to drink, which taking effect established his guilt. A rope was then tied around his neck, and by it he was dragged around the town until dead. Little did I think when visiting the head-man of that town that he could permit such barbarity, for he seemed a good natured fellow. But such is heathenism.

Not far from Good Hope Station, shortly before my first arrival on that coast, four persons were rescued from death, which was being inflicted by piecemeal. These persons were all tied to the ground so as to make it impossible for them to change their position, and fire was put to some parts of the body. One woman had fire put to her foot, another to her leg, and the only man in the company had fire put to his back. Besides this, they were in a state of actual starvation; and the first thing they requested of the missionary who effected their rescue was to give them food. To burn to death by piecemeal, with only food enough given the victim to keep life in him, is a very common mode of torturing persons for witchcraft.

One object in torturing so severely seems to be to extort confession from the victim; and with their teachings on that subject, and being distracted with pain, some confess to a crime they never committed, and for which they atone by death.

Thus many annually, because of the superstitions and cruelties of heathenism, fall victims to an indescribably painful death.

When a noted head-man dies the chief men of the town keep it a secret until they select a person to take his place, and, if possible, embezzle a part of his property. After this, they make the "cry" for him, which continues sometimes for months. If he has relatives who live at a distance, they keep the knowledge of his death from them as long as they can. This is done to save the expense of feeding them,—for all relatives coming to the "cry" must be fed at the expense of the deceased during their stay to mourn for him,—and to have the better opportunity to cheat them out of their portion of the inheritance. And that the reader may not have too exalted an opinion of the value of the estates of head-men, we will say here that, leaving out their wives, under the most favorble circumstances a few country cloths, and mats, with a crop of rice, make up the amount.

On the occasion of the death of a head-man, but not until after his interment, the people of his town go to the neighboring towns to solicit aid to defray the burial expenses; that is, to buy rum and powder to make *merry* the season allotted for *mourning*.

Where they have muskets and powder—as is

the case immediately on the coast—firing is kept up for several days after the burial takes place, and the wives and friends continue crying, or wailing, at stated times, for several weeks longer; and sometimes the whole town joins them.

Besides these, there are professional mourners, whose business it is to go from town to town for the express purpose of mourning for the dead. These must also be fed, and supplied with rum if it can be had; and they go about, especially in the night, moaning, crying, and making a most hideous noise. They call over the virtues of the deceased, often giving him more than he ever had, and then they cry out, "Oh, me sorry too much for my friend; me go hang me, me go drown me, me go kill me. Oh, me wish meself die instead of me good friend."

While I was at Good Hope Station, a man was employed to catch fish for the mission; and one night while fishing, as is common there, one of those rambling, hypocritical, drunken mourning parties came to where he was. He drank rum with them until he was intoxicated, and in that condition he came to the house at midnight, waked us all up, and was intent on having a fuss. In Africa, as in America, "when rum is in sense is out."

They "cry," or mourn, for all who die, except slaves, and persons killed in war, or for crime.

Those killed for crime are also denied a burial, and usually they are thrown into the woods to be destroyed by whatever may chance that way.

Crying for the dead is quite a business in that country; and not a few sleepless nights do missionaries spend because of the noise made by the moaning, fiddling, and drumming on such occasions. To comfort one mourning for the dead, is to "cool his heart"; and they always expect a handsome present from white persons, to assist their words of comfort "to cool their hearts."

They inter their dead by simply rolling the corpse in a mat, or cloth, and putting it under ground, sometimes near the same depth usual in this country, but often not so deep.

Just after they "pull the cry"—cease from it—for a head-man, is their favorite time to make war upon an enemy.

The notion is quite common that a noted headman can not die, but that he changes his identity, and hence they call the new head-man by the same name which the deceased had. This is also an ancient custom, so far as retaining the name is concerned. The kings of Egypt were named Pharaoh for many successive reigns.

CHAPTER XXIV.

THEOLOGY, DEVIL-WORSHIP.

Their theological views are so diversified and vague as not at all to constitute a system of doctrines and practice; and hence they have no fixed forms of worship. Some worship images of stone, which, as I suppose, were made by former generations, and kept as curiosities, or as hieroglyphical representations. They have also some wooden images. A degree of reverence is attached to these images by the people, and some say that they were made by God himself.

So far as I was able to learn, they all believe in the existence of a supreme Jehovah, who is the creator of the world, and of all things therein; that he is almighty, and just in all his ways. Some believe that the earth is his wife, and hence they sacrifice and pray to her.

They do not think that the great God concerns himself much about the affairs of men, but has committed the government and regulation of this world to inferior deities. They say, however,

AFRICAN DEVIL HOUSE.

that he will judge, and correctly decide the "palavers" of men if they importunately and perseveringly plead with him to do so when very *important* matters are in dispute.

They suppose that God is very comfortably situated in the upper world, and that he concerns himself only for his own happiness, unless something of more than common interest, among men, requires his attention and interposition.

They hold that a being whom they call devil is the author of all providence, and that he is able to bring good or ill luck upon them—especially ill luck. They attribute to him power to injure by storm, lightning, and various other means, and even to take the lives of those whose destruction he seeks. To keep on good terms with him is the main object and work of their religion; and hence they pray and sacrifice to him, with the view of deprecating his wrath and securing his friendship.

Every town has its "devil-house," or houses, where they suppose he comes, and to these they resort to offer up their sacrifices. They suppose that some "devils" run at large, while others have a particular locality, and generally in the neighborhood of a cataract, a large stone in the river, or a large tree in the forest. When they pass such places they always manifest great reverence and fear; and if they suppose the "devil" there is angry, they will sacrifice to him. Our boatmen while passing a rough place in the water said, "Devil angry too much, that make the water rough."

I saw a place on the Boom River where they had a "devil-house" in the woods, and on the top of it was a country cloth, which was put there for his use. At another time I saw them bring a quantity of rice and palm-oil, and place them near the "devil-house." They often take the best food they have, prepared in the best order, and give it, as they say, to the "devil" to eat. They suppose him to be of similar tastes to themselves; and hence such articles of food as they relish they give to him. At another time I saw them put a quantity of rice in an iron pot, which was sunk into the ground its whole depth, being near the "devil-place." Upon inquiry what that was for, they said the "devil" would come into the pot and tell them what witch trouble their friends if they get sick.

Near the Wela Falls, on the Jong River, Mr. Brooks and I were passing a "devil-house," under which, among other things, lay a beautiful round stone, about the size of a potato, which I took up to look at. For doing this I was called to an account by the head-men of Wela; and after much "palaver" with them, Mr. B. bought me off for the value of forty-eight cents, and a piece of lead, which they said they would give the "devil" to appease his wrath, who was now very angry because of what I had done. They wanted silver; but that being refused, they said lead would do if they would cut off the outside and make it shine like silver, for the "devil" would then think it was silver, and would not know the difference. We thought with them, that lead would do as well as silver, and be cheaper for us.

These "devil-houses" are mostly mere open sheds, being from three to four feet square, and of about the same height. Under them they often have pieces of china-ware, and glass, or something of the kind. If they can get from white men what they can not make themselves, if only broken glass, they regard it so sacred as to be worthy a place in the "devil-house," which seems to be a favorite depository for things which they regard as beautiful and valuable.

They are emphatically devil-worshipers; and they are most profoundly selfish in their worship, as in most other things. We must not forget, however, that in their present condition they are not capable of exercising other than selfish motives. They have no systematic form of worship, but differ in this as much as people do in America.

They evince most clearly that "man is a religious animal," and, as might be supposed, in the absence of divine revelation or any guide to direct them, they are deeply sunken in idolatry, superstition, and selfishness. They demonstrate the declaration that the thoughts and the imaginations of men are evil continually.

The only reason why our theological views are not as foolish and corrupting as theirs, and that we are not believers in witchcraft, devil-worship, and a thousand other foolish things, is simply because the light of Heaven shines upon us. How soon would all the impositions and cruelties found among heathens be practiced by us, were the restraints of Christianity removed. Without these, ours would be a more powerful and efficient machinery for the promotion of all that is debasing and cruel.

The time was when people were killed in this country for the imaginary crime of witchcraft, and by those, too, whom we are proud to call our forefathers. But as light increased belief in witches ceased, and with it the cruelties growing out of that belief. Witches and hobgoblins never flourish in the light of a pure gospel. Were the day and Sabbath schools in the United States closed, religious services discontinued, and Bibles removed from our midst, a half century would not pass before witchcraft and numerous other superstitious practices would be common here.

AFRICAN GREGREES.

CHAPTER XXV.

GREGREES.

The superstitions of the people afford them a ready explanation for many things otherwise mysterious to them, and yet explainable upon natural principles by an enlightened mind. They believe that the power of the gregree, the work of witches, and the doings of evil spirits produce many phenomena in the physical world which are the results of natural causes.

Gregrees are of different sizes and shapes, and of various kinds of material. Mohammedans make a great many, though they are made by pagans also. A Mohammedan gregree is a piece of paper, with a few Arabic letters and characters upon it, incased in leather or cloth. When used it is suspended to some part of the body, usually the neck. A pagan gregree is a few leaves, or a little clay, or sand, or a pebble, or bark of a tree, incased in a cloth, or tied together. It is fastened to the wrists, ankles, and other parts of the body.

They suppose these will keep off disease, and the intended injuries of enemies; preserve from poisonous serpents, and wild animals; keep off all evil, and secure all good.

Gregrees are so common that few persons are without at least one; and sometimes ten, and even twenty are found upon the same individual. Ordinarily each one has a particular office to fill, in the way of averting evil and producing good; but some of them, like patent medicines of this country, *are good for everything.* Confidence in them is most degrading to the intellect; and besides, it gives great scope to the impostures of those who make them. Exorbitant prices are demanded; sometimes the value of several slaves for one. Once I asked an intelligent heathen what good he derived from his gregrees. He said those on his ankles would keep snakes from "bite" him, and those on his wrists and neck would keep "bad sick from catch him."

At Baily, after staying over night, the company consisting of four missionaries, the head-man of the town asked us to give him a piece of silver. He had treated us kindly, had given us presents, and we could not well deny his request. After we had given him the silver we inquired what he intended to do with it. He told us he wanted to make "war sarica" with it—which is a charm that secures from war. He said that all the people of the town would meet together and lay their hands upon the money, and in the meantime one of his great men would make a speech, showing the benefits of the charm. The money would then be incased in cloth, and deposited in a safe place; "and this," said he, "make that no war come to my town."

They also have "war cooks," whose business it is to tell where war may be carried on successfully. Sometimes they get their power of divination by putting different vegetables and various kinds of leaves into a pot of water, and boiling them. Then by looking into the stained water they pretend to tell—whether by the color of the water or otherwise I can not tell—where an army will be victorious.

These cooks are generally Mohammedans; and as they mostly speak, read, and write Arabic, by correspondence with each other they can easily defeat or make victorious the party they may select, for they have the entire control of the armies of the people who employ them, and being more intelligent than head-men generally are, they impose upon them shockingly.

The Mohammedans, by the power of these "war cooks," and various other stratagems, not a few in number, have acquired the ascendency in many places which but a few years since were under the control of real pagans. Indeed all the Mohammedan chiefs in the Sherbro and Mendi countries are usurpers, and hold their towns not by right, but by might. They manage to put down or out of the way—by administering poison, if nothing else will do,—those who have much influence in the country. It is thought that King Peer-Charly, and others, who died while I was in Africa, were poisoned by their doctors who were Mohammedans.

Gregrees afford security from all evil, and give the necessary instruction in all cases of emergency. They are emphatically their light in darkness, their wisdom in ignorance, and their strength in weakness. In them they find a balm for every wound, and a remedy for all the ills of life. In short, they put more confidence in them than many professors of religion do in the Bible, and the God of the Bible.

Once I asked the head-man of a town what he would take for a witch gregree, which at the time was hanging near the door-way of his hut. He looked at me with surprise, and said, with his voice elevated, "You *want to take my witch-medicine away so witch come and kill me* ONE TIME." Another time, when on the river, my men seemed much alarmed upon the water growing rough, because of an approaching storm, and when I inquired the cause of their fear, one replied they had no gregree for storm on water.

I brought several kinds of gregrees with me to this country, and one "country fashion." The country fashion is about four inches long, three inches wide, and two inches thick. It is covered with cloth, and has some Arabic characters in it. This is used for a variety of things—such as driving evil spirits out of town, trying convicts, curing the sick, and keeping off sickness.

To try convicts, the gregree-man rubs this on a piece of board, or wood, back and forward, and so long as he can keep it going, the accused is accounted innocent, but if it stops he is guilty. They believe that some supernatural power holds back, or makes powerless the hand of the operator, so that he can not continue to move the country fashion, if the accused be guilty, while the truth is he may cease to move it at pleasure. Surely that "people is destroyed for lack of knowledge."

I must give some account of a few of the gregrees I brought from Africa. Two of them were taken from a slave canoe which was captured, and the slaves liberated. One was to tell whether slave-canoes could pass places where there was a liability to be captured. They have a way of consulting them to learn such things from them. The captain of the canoe here spoken of was told by his gregree that if he would take a little girl, and hold her foot in a pot of boiling water, he could pass a point of danger safely. Just after passing that place he and his slaves were taken, with the little girl still on board; but the flesh had all fallen off the boiled foot! She died subsequently. The gregree also told him that after he had passed the place he must sacrifice a slave to the devil, for granting him such good luck. This victim had already been selected, and but for the capture of the canoe would have been killed in a short time. The other gregree taken from that canoe "was good to keep sick from catching the captain."

The third one is simply an old padlock covered with cloth, having some of the virtue-giving Arabic writing inclosed. This will cause its owner to have plenty of money, and no one would refuse to trust him if he wished to buy anything. In that country it is customary to pay part, at least, in advance for labor and goods; but this gregree would give others such confidence in its owner that they would trust him for all. Doubtless the old lock was begged or stolen from some trader, and because it served as a safeguard to keep money in a chest, house, or wherever they saw it used, they concluded that it would, with a little Arabic writing, be good to bring money in, and cause others to wait for money due them.

Another of these gregrees is simply a roll of splinters, with some of the efficacious writing in the inside; and "this good" to keep witches out of houses, and from hurting persons anywhere. This class of gregrees is very numerous. With but few if any exceptions, all feel the need of protection from the injury which witches are sure to bring upon them unless they are thus secured.

It is truly remarkable how confidently they believe these gregrees will produce the results for which they are used; and though they have been deceived by them scores of times, they still cling to them most firmly.

If any one makes a new discovery, performs an extraordinary feat, or is very skillful in any respect whatever, they say "he have some gregree for show that." I heard one say that the reason white people know so much, and make so many fine things, is because they have "one *big*, BIG gregree for show them."

The English consul of Sherbro Island, Rev. Mr. Handsen, some years since, captured two slave-canoes at the same time, having only his boatmen, some six or seven men, to assist him. He shot the leader of the canoes, and then rushed suddenly upon the others, frightening them into non-resistance and submission.

After the slaves were released, a number of them gathered around the consul's boat, looked upon him with admiration and surprise, and said, '*Big*, BIG medicine live in that boat." They thought what he did was by the power of the gregree, supposing that such success could not attend him without one.

CHAPTER XXVI.

CREATION OF MAN.

What has been said in the preceding pages concerning gregrees will prepare the mind of the reader to form some idea of the views of the work of creation in general, and the creation of man in particular, entertained by the Africans.

On this subject I need here only narrate a legend current among the Mendi tribe, illustrative of the order God observed in man's creation, and the reason of the difference existing between different tribes of people. The story runs thus: "God made white man early in the morning, and take plenty time to show him book palaver [how to read], and God palaver [a knowledge of the gospel], and how to make plenty fine things. Then he tell him to go.

"Next he make Mohammedan man, and show him little book palaver, and how to make some fine things [most all that is manufactured in that country that exhibits skill, Mohammedans make]; and then he tell him go to.

"After this he make Mendi man, and showed him how to farm, make country cloth, mats, canoes, and such like things; and then he tell him to go.

"In the last place, he make Sherbro man; and when he get him done the sun go down, and he had no time to show him anything but make salt and catch fish, but promised to come back and show him more things. But he forgot to do so, and that the reason Sherbro man know so little."

Some of the Timiny tribe say that the reason why white people are superior to their race in this world is, because they choose their good things here, but black man choose his good things in the next world. God offered both happiness in the next world, if they would be content to brook hardships in this; but white man said he wanted his good things now, and hence God gave them.

Dear reader, ought not you and I to praise God with our lips, and in our lives, that we may have good things in the present and in the future world? "No good thing will he withhold from them that walk uprightly." Oh! the unspeakable goodness of God, and the condescension of Christ "in giving himself for us, that he might redeem us from all iniquity and purify unto himself a peculiar people zealous of good works." Are we that peculiar people, and are we zealous of good works? If so we will not hold our peace, nor rest, until the darkened sons and daughters of Africa, who think they are necessarily compelled to drag out lives of wretchedness, enjoy the same opportunities of being happy that we possess, both in this and in the world to come.

CHAPTER XXVII.

FUTURE STATE.

Africans generally believe in a future state of being; but their views of that state are very different. The Timinies speak of "good die," and "bad die" meaning that some die happy, and others miserable. They also speak of "good live, and "bad live" in eternity—meaning that some will be happy there, while others will be unhappy.

Some of the Mendi tribe believe that persons will sustain the same relation to each other in eternity that they do in this life; that those who are head-men here will be head-men there, and those who are slaves here will be slaves in the future world. In view of this belief, a head-man on the Boom River, during my stay in Africa, sent a company of men to make war upon a town to kill slaves for his son, who had been killed in a previous engagement by the people of that town. His people met with a second defeat; and when they came back and told the old man what had happened he flew into a rage, and said to his men, "Me no care if you no go kill my enemies to be slaves for my son, then let my enemies kill you and you go and be slaves for him." The main object was to get persons to serve his son in eternity, and he would a little rather have his enemies killed for that purpose; but if that could not be done, then he was willing his own people should be sacrificed for that object.

Some suppose that those who die return into the world again in a state of infancy. In that case the gregree-man is called upon the birth of a child, to say who has returned to be an inhabitant of earth again; and when this matter is settled, the child is named after that person. They all seem to think that the spirit of the deceased lingers for some time near the spot where the body was when the spirit left it, and some have a great dread to enter the house where a person has recently died.

Some also think that the soul, like the body, requires food until it undergoes some change, which change they say does not take place until some time after death.

Because of this belief they cook rice, and whatever else they eat themselves,—which is mostly rice and palm-oil,—and place it upon the graves of their deceased friends. I saw this done at York

Island, and at other places. They believe that the spirits of the deceased come out of their graves and eat the food put there. The country abounds with birds and fowls, and many hungry children are always on the alert for something to eat, and hence the food disappears in a short time; and those stupid creatures take this as evidence that their departed friends eat it. They think they are conferring a great favor upon them in furnishing them food.

CHAPTER XXVIII.

SLAVERY, SLAVE-TRADE.

Slavery deserves notice as a African institution. This institution in Africa, as for more than two centuries in America, is "the sum of all villainies," and to such an extent is this system of villainy carried on, that it is supposed by some that two thirds of the entire population of that country are slaves to the other third.

Slavery and the domestic slave-trade in Africa, as they were in America, are the prolific sources of infinite suffering; alike in their general features, cursing both master and slave.

When slaves are taken from one place to another, they are packed into canoes as sacks of grain are put into wagons in this country; and thus, with little or no food, they are often left for several days together.

The customs and laws of that country, as in slave states, bear the cruel impress of slavery, and certain classes of free people have no security that their liberties will be continued them. Is one poor, or in debt, or unfortunate, or a thief, or surety for another and can not pay; or does one curse the king—speaking against him, though it may be *justly*, is *cursing him*, and punishable just as speaking against slavery, though ever so *mildly* and *justly*, was punishable in the South, and by the laws of slave states, when slavery existed in them; or is he found in suspicious circumstances; or does he profane a sacred place, or a religious rite,—for any of the above named things he may be sold into slavery, unless he has the uncommon good fortune to have friends to interpose in his behalf. Is a wife untrue, she is often sold into slavery. Is a father in straightened circumstances, he pawns his child, with no hope, often, of being able to redeem that child.

The system of involuntary servitude is an evil, socially, intellectually, politically, and morally, in Africa, as in every other country where it exists. Out of it grow fearful cruelties; and perhaps a more fit appellation can not be given it than to call it the *emblem of hell*.

The Soosoos, who occupy the country north of Sierra Leone, are the great slave-traders and slave-owners. They often stint their slaves in food, and work them very hard on their ground-nut plantations. The country south-east of Sierra Leone, for many miles on the coast, is to them what Virginia formerly was to the sugar-growing states of this confederacy, namely, the slave-growing region. It was thought that in the year 1855 not less than seventy slave-canoes, with cargoes, passed through the lagoon which divides Sherbro Island from the mainland, *en route* for the Soosoo country. A number of canoes were also taken; but as they travel mostly by night, and have a great many places in which to secrete themselves by day all along the coast, many avoid detection.

From twenty to forty are packed into one canoe—put into the closest possible space as a matter of course. In this condition they often get sick; but they are not cared for any more than a sick dog would be of the same value. How similar to the treatment of slaves by white men.

In evidence of this, we will give the treatment which a cargo of slaves taken on board in that country, and landed at the West Indies, received at the hands of white men, and a white captain. We have this from the captain's own lips. In two hours eight hundred slaves were put into the vessel—in his own words, "tumbled into the hold like sacks of grain." On the passage, three hundred died. The only attention paid to the sick was to remove the dead from among them every morning. Some mornings thirty were thrown overboard. So great was the stench coming from the hold when the hatches were opened that none could endure it long. Perhaps none but crews of slave-vessels would have endured it at all. On the passage a man was kept at the top of the mainmast all the time to look out for cruisers and other vessels, so as to avoid detection. The vessel came near being taken by a man-of-war on the American coast, and was kept from taking on board the cargo of slaves for six weeks, by a man-of-war on the African coast.

After the slaves were landed, the vessel was burned; but with the loss of it, and of the three hundred slaves on the passage, five thousand dollars were still cleared for the owners. The captain was offered great wages to make a second trip, but refused, giving as a reason, that he could not be so inhuman, so utterly sold to cruelty, as those of necessity must be who traffic in slaves on the high seas. He also told me that he was closely pursued by officers in this country, and would have been taken in all probability had he not fled to another.

The only reason why I refer to this circumstance is to show that cruelty is inseparably connected with the system of slavery, and that for gain white men are quite as inhuman as are African heathens. The love of power and money, connected with the system of slavery, has wrung groans, tears, and blood from many who were "created in the image of God." "Man's inhumanity to man causes countless millions to mourn."

Through the influence of the Mendi and Sherbro missions and the vigilance of the officers of the colony of Sierra Leone, and of traders and missionaries generally, the traffic in slaves has been largely suppressed—on the west coast especially, in the country where our own mission is located. It has of late become so difficult to get their slaves away without being detected, arrested, and punished, that few persons are now willing to take the risks which are necessarily connected with it.

CHAPTER XXIX.

PURROW-BUSH SOCIETY.

Next a chapter will be given on the doings of the " Purrow-bush," sometimes called "Devil-bush Society." Of all the doings of this society I am unable to speak; but this I know, that it is a *secret society*, and among its distinguishing peculiarities are sworn opposition to every system of religion and government contrary to their own, and the promotion of idolatry and amuletism among the people. As before stated, the people are " devil-worshipers;" and there can be little doubt that this society was organized for the more systematic and zealous worship of Satan. It holds its meetings near the spot where Satan is supposed to have at least a temporary residence, or a favored stopping-place, and over which he exerts, as they suppose, a powerful influence.

A certain initiatory ceremony is observed, and the name of the applicant is altered when admitted into the society.

This mystic order, besides regulating the worship of the people, commerce, and the value of things generally, infuses into the minds of the common people sentiments detrimental to the spread of Christianity. To my certain knowledge, the "purrow society" prevented the Mendi missionaries from commencing a mission-station at Wela. The head-man of that town, its inhabitants, and a large portion of the people immediately thereabouts, wished it done. By permission of the head-man and of the people most interested in the place, the brethren of that mission had some vegetables and fruit-trees planted there, and a man employed to take care of them. But this society put "purrow law" upon the place, the substance of which is, that no one must do anything there, either directly or indirectly, unless they do it "*by strong,*"—by resisting and overcoming the forces of those putting the "purrow laws" there, or by war.

This society engenders pride and selfishness, and is the means in the hands of Satan of leading its members and advocates farther into wickedness. When one joins the purrow he looks down with contempt upon those who do not belong to the society. A negro who helped navigate our boat a number of trips became a member of this society while in our employ, and the change in his conduct toward myself and others was so marked that we often spoke of it at the time

Women are not allowed to belong to the society, or to be on the ground where it meets; and when they walk out of the town during the society's meetings they are required to clap their hands together, so as to make a noise, that they may be warned by the sentinel on guard not to go farther in the direction leading to the place of meeting.

Had one of their own women done what I did at the "purrow-bush house," near the falls of Jong River,—which was simply to take into my hands a round stone which lay in the house,—she would have lost her life; and for the same offense one of their own men who is not a member of the society would have been sold into slavery.

Mr. Brooks, who had an excellent faculty for the investigation of such matters, being a man of quick perception and keen insight into human nature, and who had long resided in that country, and had obtained a great influence over the people in general, and the members of the "purrow society" in particular, and who had taken special pains to collect facts concerning this society, sketched a history of its doings, from which we extract the following concerning their meetings:

"One of the members of this association acts in the capacity of a devil. He speaks through a trumpet, made of a bottle with a hole in the neck like a flute. He also has an interpreter, who is privy to all the wishes of the "purrow;" and he speaks what they wish, and not what is spoken by the trumpet. What the man with the trumpet says must be done is done, even to the taking of life. No woman is allowed to see either the trumpet or the man using it; and if she should, she must die. A boy who strolls into the woods where they meet is generally detained, and introduced into all the superstitions of the purrow. All the people in the purrow, or devil's belly, as they call their place of meeting, must '*cook* for the devil."

It is a remarkable fact that circumcision is also one of the rites of this order. My antisecret, as also my antislavery, principles were strengthened by an acquaintance with these institutions in Africa. The church and the world would be better without them.

There are several other secret societies in that country, some composed of men solely, and others of women. Their names and operations are briefly given in a subsequent chapter of this volume.

CHAPTER XXX.

CONDITION AND WANTS OF THE PEOPLE.

It is almost impossible to conceive of a condition more wretched, and more to be deplored, than that of the people of western Africa. It is in every way wretched, physically, intellectually, and morally, and still, alas! their course is steadily downward; and this downward tendency is greatly accelerated by influences emanating from men hailing from enlightened and professedly Christian nations, as we shall see in a subsequent chapter of this volume.

They need an entire set of new institutions, social, educational, political, and religious—a complete regeneration; and that this may be effected it is essential that good and wise people go among them, to lay the basis of correct society, and introduce the arts and sciences.

I would not be understood to convey the idea that this end should be aimed at in any other way than by the introduction of the gospel in their midst, but rather as the result of the gospel, which result always follows when its truths are received and obeyed.

The Africans possess, in an eminent degree, the following two prominent features of character, namely, faith and obedience. With them the mysterious and miraculous enter largely into the character of the Supreme Jehovah; and hence, when they obtain an intelligent view of Christianity the glorious miracles of the Bible are readily believed, and are highly appreciated. It is comparatively easy for them to believe the Holy Scriptures, and exercise faith in the Savior of men. By faith here I do not mean presumption, but real, living, soul-saving faith, such as God requires as a condition of justification.

They are also a *submissive* people, and are susceptible of the deepest *feeling*, which, when regulated by the grace of God in their hearts, makes them zealous in the cause of Christianity. But they must be taught the way of salvation; and this will infuse, more than anything else, energy and enterprise, and thus cause temporal prosperity to spring up among them.

CHAPTER XXXI.

ENCOURAGEMENTS TO LABOR.

From the experiment already made in the colony of Sierra Leone, we are fully warranted in the assertion that missionaries have a great influence over that people for good, and that they may do much to elevate them from a state of degradation to a state of moral purity. True, there yet remains much to be done where missionaries have operated for years; but is there not also much to be done yet among the people of this country, who have heard the gospel, and have had its restraining and purifying influences thrown around them from childhood?

Some half-hearted religionists, and wicked persons who neither fear God nor regard the rights of man, there will be, in despite of all that Christianity can do to prevent it. Were all the clergymen of Ohio to concentrate their efforts in one county, and were they all much better men than most of them now are, still some of the people of that county would live and die in sin.

Paul understood this; and hence, when he had planted a church and fully declared the whole gospel in one place he went to another; and thus he continued to go about much of his time, kindling up the glorious light of the gospel that men *might* be saved if they *would*. The argument that we have sinners enough at home, "stay here and preach instead of going to Africa," is worth nothing at all. True, we must keep up the institutions of Christianity at home, or in a few centuries we should be what the Africans are now in point of moral degradation; but we must also do our duty in sending the gospel to those who have it not. We should be encouraged in the prosecution of this work,

First: From the success which has attended the labors of those who have been and are still employed in it. In the colony of Sierra Leone many of the colored people have comfortable and well-furnished houses—dress decently, and even elegantly. An ample fortune has been attained by numbers, by their own exertions. A knowledge of such trades as are needed in that country has been obtained. Among them are found shoemakers, tailors, blacksmiths, carpenters, masons, painters, watch-makers, and others.

The colony is well supplied with week-day and Sabbath-schools, conducted by colored teachers; and it has also quite a number of clergymen who were raised up in it, some of whom reflect honor upon their calling. I am not blind to the manifold wants still existing within the colony, but when it is compared with those places where heathenism reigns undisturbed, there is reason for rejoicing in the great work that has been effected. Many sincere Christians are there; and some have died in the faith, and have gone to heaven. We might refer to other places on the coast. And indeed we need not go outside of Sherbro Mission to obtain abundant proof that the labor of missionaries among that people is not in vain. No one can go into the schools of that mission without being strongly impressed with the improvement the pupils have made in the acquisition of knowledge, and in the change of manners. And then there are some whose conversion from heathenism to Christianity has been shown to be genuine by their consistent, upright lives for years past.

Second: The promises of God afford great encouragement to missionary effort in Africa. "Ethiopia shall stretch out her hands to God." "Ask of me, and I shall give thee the heathen for thine inheritance, and the uttermost parts of the earth for thy possession." "Lo, I am with you alway, even unto the end of the world." God has not only promised to be with his servants when they go to show the heathen the way of salvation, but he has also promised them success. Where have the servants of the Most High labored perseveringly without reaping a harvest of souls of precious value?

Judson and others toiled and waited for years before they saw the fruit of their labors; but such was their faith that they felt assured that God would in his own time water the seed sown, and cause it to bring forth fruit in the salvation of souls. God is faithful concerning his promises, and he will most assuredly fulfill them. "Faithful is he that calleth" us to the prosecution of this great and glorious work, and he will do it! Who can doubt the certain accomplishment of the work which God has so positively declared should be done?

Third: We ought to be encouraged to labor to enlighten heathens, not only because of past success, and the promise of this in the future, but also because it is our bounden duty to do so. "Go ye into all the world, and preach the gospel to every creature." An important part of the work of the church is to enlarge her borders,—give those the light of the gospel who have it not, and bring them under the saving influence of the grace of God. "Let your light so shine before men, that they may see your good works, and glorify your Father which is in heaven." We can not let our light shine before men in Africa unless we go there. Admit the Bible as our guide, and our duty is plain.

CHAPTER XXXII.

THE VICIOUS INFLUENCE OF THE WHITES.

I shall now show that the treatment which that people have received from the people of Europe and America places us under lasting obligations to them. If *restitution* is a part of repentance, which we most firmly believe, when it lies in the power of the trespasser to make it to the injured, then we can never receive pardon at the hands of God for wrongs inflicted upon the African race, except we make to them all the restitution which lies within our power. What has been our conduct toward that race?

First: We had, up to the commencement of the last century, robbed Africa of no less than twenty-five millions of people by the inhuman slave-trade alone. The history of the slave-trade is written in characters of blood! Could the dead on the shores of Africa, and those who found a watery grave in the briny deep, and many on American soil, who came to a premature death by the slave-trade, testify of the sufferings they endured, we would be filled with horror, and almost hate our race. But the injury done them involved vastly more than loss of life and physical sufferings. Other results, quite as prolific of suffering and injustice, grew out of the slave-trade.

To get a cargo of flesh, bone, and blood the trader would say to the head-man of a town, or the king of a country, "You get me so many slaves, and I will give you so much powder, tobacco, and rum." To obtain them, war was made upon some weak, defenseless town in the night, and the required number captured.

Thus petty wars were instigated, which to this day are carried on by some of the tribes for the procurement of slaves. By slave-traders the elements of hell were introduced; and they have been kept in motion, and still cause murder and rapine, with cruel and bloody hands and insatiate maw, to walk through that dark land, diffusing everywhere distrust, hate, and misery.

I will not further detail the injuries done them by the slave-traffic, for their name is legion. But if the blood of Abel cried to God from the ground for vengeance, surely the tears and blood which have been shed, and which are still being poured out in Africa on account of this inhuman traffic, are crying to God with a voice louder than thunder. And think you, reader, that this catalogue of crimes, so fearful and black, will go unpunished? "Will not the Judge of all the earth do right?" Guilty one, rest not easy. "Because sentence against an evil work is not executed speedily," do not "have your heart fully set in you to do evil." "Vengence is mine; I will repay, saith the Lord." If you have, either directly or indirectly, by your influence or by your vote, encouraged the holding of slaves or the traffic in them in any shape whatever, are you clear of the blood of men?

Second: Much has been done to degrade the people by the use of ardent spirits among them. Go where you will in heathen countries, and you may find the white man's rum and tobacco, and indeed, almost every vice, and vice-producer of enlightened countries.

Let those who try to screen themselves from the guilt of making ardent spirits, and who take to themselves praise because they do not keep a rum-shop on the ground where they distill the liquor, but barrel it up and send it to market without havng any drank, or any injured by it, remember that the damning effects of their distilleries are fearfully felt in Africa and all heathen countries, as well as in others. Think you that the Africans are better qualified to handle such a dangerous article with discretion, and without abusing it, than you are? If with all the restraints of the Bible and the frowns of public sentiment against the habitual use of ardent spirits as a beverage there is danger of being overcome and destroyed by it in this land, as multiplied thousands are, then the liability of being ruined by it, soul and body, where all these checks are unknown, must be vastly greater. Is not a dangerous weapon safer in the hands of an enlightened person, who at least should have control over himself, and whose position in society throws around him a powerfully restraining influence, than in the hands of one who is already low in vice, and who has nothing to lose by a misuse, or the careless use of that weapon?

Third: The frauds and cruelties practiced by traders from enlightened countries have done much to increase the wickedness of the people. New ways of sinning have been taught them, and new temptations have been placed before them. All know how wicked and designing men wrong their fellows in this country, and how trying it is to the better and finer feelings of our nature to be imposed upon and cheated.

We may conceive how easily advantage may be taken of the ignorance and weakness of a superstitious people, and that the most shameful frauds may be practiced upon them. Numerous instances might be mentioned to show that this has been done; but we shall dismiss the subject by saying that up to this time, though there is more competition now than ever before, and the people have more knowledge of the value of all articles taken there in exchange for their produce than at any former period, yet on some articles the trader makes a profit of many times the original cost of them.

CHAPTER XXXIII.

WHAT JUSTICE DEMANDS, GOD COMMANDS.

Now, if those from enlightened countries and of our own color have done so much to debase that people, ought we not to do something to elevate them? Can justice demand less than this at our hands? And is it not a reasonable demand? Fellow-citizen, philanthropist, and Christian, what response do you make to these interrogations? If there is a race of people on earth that should draw from us sympathy and benevolent deeds, that race is the African. For my part, I can not explain how we can be guiltless in the sight of high heaven unless we put forth our hands to raise them from the dreadful condition into which we placed them? Is it not to be feared that the Savior will say to us, "Inasmuch as ye did it not unto one of the least of these, ye did it not unto me?"

We are commanded to do good to all men as we have opportunity; and our opportunity to do that people good is favorable. But to accomplish that good, sacrifices must be made, not only of money, but also of friends, health, and life it may be. Many must leave their native land and go among them. Persons of different vocations should go. The farmer and the mechanic, as well as the school-teacher and preacher, if they be God-fearing persons, may do valuable service in the great work contemplated. If we are "crucified to the world, and the world to us," if we are denying ourselves and following Christ, or if we are *Christians*, we will be willing to go to Africa if the Lord so direct us.

At least all ministers are willing to go who have entered the ministry with a clear understanding of the import of the commission Christ gave the apostles just before his ascent into heaven, which commission is just as binding on the present ministry as it was on the apostles. When the Savior said, "Lo, I am with you alway, even to the end of the world," he could not have meant that the apostles should live to the end of time, but he meant that after their decease others should be called to the ministry, and still others, and that to the end of the world there should be a Christ-attended ministry. Hence it is as much our duty to "go and teach all nations, baptizing them in the name of the Father, and of the Son, and of the Holy Ghost," as it was the duty of those who heard these words fall from the lips of the blessed Christ. But in order to teach the nations we must go where they are. If we are the willing servants of the "Most High," we are ready to go where the providence of God directs. We had better be in Africa with the fever six months out of twelve, than to be out of the line of duty. We will be happier in suffering the loss of all things for Christ's sake, than in the possession of all things if disobedient.

External circumstances have little to do with happiness; for God can and does overrule privation and affliction, and make them sources of happiness to his faithful servants. No man can be unhappy while he obeys God.

CHAPTER XXXIV.

MEASURE AND TEST OF LOVE.

I must be permitted to dwell for a few moments upon a subject on which the Scriptures are plain and unequivocal; but it is a subject which the Christian world is slow to comprehend and appreciate. It is the relation which money and personal sacrifice sustain to the evangelization of the heathen. Turn to I. John iii. 16, 17.

In the sixteenth verse the idea of self-sacrifice is presented, and a sacrifice is required which is more valuable than all the wealth that it has ever yet been the fortune of any mortal to possess,—for "*all that a man hath will he give for his life;*" and here he is called *to give his life*, if the promotion of Christ's cause demands it.

In the seventeenth verse worldly goods are spoken of, and the strong implication is that those who withhold them can not enjoy the love of God.

Connect this with a parallel passage in Ephesians, v. 5, where it is said that the covetous man

—who is an idolater—" hath no inheritance in the kingdom of Christ and of God;" and the case is fully made out that covetous persons are not the subjects of the kingdom of grace on earth, nor will they be possessors of the kingdom of heaven above.

Those ministers of the gospel, then, who send covetous people to perdition land them *not far* from the place where the Bible lets *them* down; and if the Bible is reliable testimony in the case, then the idolater has as good a chance for heaven without praying as the covetous professor of religion has without paying, with all the praying and weeping he can do. One of the texts quoted denies him the love of God in this world, and the other denies him admission into heaven; and more than this can not be denied the thief, or the profaner of God's name. "*If any man love the world, the love of the Father is not in him.*"

Now read slowly and reflectingly. "Hereby perceive we the love of God, because he laid down his life for us: and we ought to lay down our lives for the brethren. But whoso hath this world's good, and seeth his brother have need, and shutteth up his bowels of compassion from him, how dwelleth the love of God in him?"

Some say we ought to give the tenth; and what an improvement in our contributions would be apparent if all would give this much! But the New Testament knows no such definite rule, no such exact limit. It does not intimate that we may stop at the tenth. The gospel idea is, that we are to give when objects of need present themselves to us, *as our ability* will allow.

"Whoso *hath* this world's good." Nothing is said of the amount he has, or of the proportion he is to give. If a man has two farms and sells one, and gives the proceeds thereof to benevolent purposes, and an object of charity—a "brother in need"—then presents himself to that man, and he can give without impoverishing his family, or those dependent on him for support, he is *still* bound to give. Many *who have no real estate* give, —and as a general thing those are the most benevolent. Surely, then, the man with *one farm*, though he may have given twenty farms away before, should still give. The only questions are, *Has he "this world's good?"* and, *Is there a "brother in need?"*—in need of temporal or spiritual blessings, whether he be white, black, or red, living in America, Asia, or Africa. If there is, *he must give.*

If we take the primitive Christians for a standard by which to regulate giving we shall find ourselves wofully deficient, for they *sold all that they had* and laid the proceeds at the apostles' feet; and distribution was made unto every man according as he had need. If it be true that all that we have and are is Christ's, might it not also be *our* duty to give all for the promotion of his kingdom?

But if we *take the Savior* as an example of benevolence, we will carry on the work of evangelization at any and every cost. He left a better residence, in a better country, and better friends than it is possible for us to leave, and came into as bad a place, and among as bad a people as is possible for us to find; for nowhere would the people do worse than kill us. He gave up his wealth in heaven, and then his life a ransom for us.

Concerning the African mission, many reason thus:

"It will cost too much; and besides, it will do no good. They are a stupid, degraded people anyhow, and there can nothing be made out of them. Go among them and do all you can to teach them better, and they will rob you of your goods, and keep on doing as they now do. God has placed them over there in Africa, and he will do right with them. Stay at home and do good here, and don't go over there and get sick and die."

Now the blessed Savior in heaven could have said as bad things of the people living on earth just before he came to this world, as can be said of the Africans; but still he came, and let them abuse and kill him, and rob him of all he had for the sake of unbarring heaven's gate to them. Had he done as many do toward the heathen, we would have sunk to utter ruin.

We are absolutely commanded to do to others as we would have them do to us; and were we in their condition, and they in ours, would we not desire them to give us the gospel? And by so doing we will at the same time enhance our own happiness, both in time and eternity. It is a truth established by experience, observation, and scripture that those who do most for the extension of Christ's kingdom among men enjoy most of the Divine presence in this life; and that such will be very happy in death and in heaven there can be no doubt.

Dying men have complained, and even those who were thought to be excellent men and devoted Christians, that they had not done enough for God and his cause; but we have never heard of one who regretted that he had done too much.

As Christians, we are to improve the talents God has given us, and the money talent of the Church is of such a character that, if improved by us, we may under God accomplish an important work in the great enterprise of evangelization. The Church has the *means* and MEN, which if consecrated and used are able to spread the gospel far and wide, but which if unconsecrated and unimproved may be taken away.

The history of the church in every age of the world is evidence to the point. Take as an example the Jewish people. They were prospered only so long as they were faithful to the charge intrusted to them, but when they became penurious and offered blemished sacrifices to God, instead of the best of their flocks, as they were commanded to do, their glory departed from them, and they became poor,—and especially poor in religious life, as is now the case with the close-fisted professor of religion. He that soweth sparingly shall also reap sparingly, but he that soweth bountifully shall also reap bountifully. God can cause a certain spot of ground, or business, to yield a hundred dollars profit, which if given *to Him* will secure the donor at least one thousand dollars worth of happiness; but if withheld from him, He will withhold the happiness, and *may* afterward withhold the increase or gain.

There are wicked men whom the Lord lets alone, as he did Ephraim. They are joined to the idol of wealth; and the Lord permits them to make all the money they can, and do with it what they please. And many such become rich. God knows they will have a hard time of it in the world to come, where, like the rich man spoken of by the Savior, they may be denied water to cool their tongues; and he lets them enjoy their idol while here on earth.

But the case is different with persons of enlightened consciences, who have tasted that God is good, and who, though they may have lost it, once possessed the pardoning love of God in their hearts. Such persons are prepared to appreciate the blessings of salvation to some extent, at least; and hence they must feel the importance of "giving as the Lord hath prospered them," to send the gospel, with its untold blessings, to those who have it not. Such will be cursed often in their basket and store, if they withhold. Why is it that so many people, though they make money, and never give any away, still do not prosper?

How often do professors of religion say that they would not give their hope of heaven for all the world, and yet refuse a very small amount of their part of the world to give others that same hope of heaven. If the hope of heaven is so valuable, and puts them in possession of joy inexpressible and abiding, think you not that it will be of as much value to that dark African, whose mind is still darker than his skin, as it is to them? That a well-grounded hope of heaven is of more value to an individual than all the world would be, is certainly true; but that those who are so close-fisted as to refuse a respectable portion of their means, to put within the reach of the heathen the same hope, are in possession of a well-founded hope of heaven, is certainly a mistake.

"I speak as unto wise men; judge ye what I say."

CHAPTER XXXV.

WHAT THE GOSPEL WILL DO.

I assume what I suppose will not be denied by a Christian, that the gospel will do for all heathens what it has done for us; and hence I shall only give a brief sketch of the blessings flowing from the gospel to us, as a nation, to show what it will do for those who have it not. That we are indebted to Christianity for all that we possess above heathens, no Christian will deny. To it we are indebted for a free government, which in itself is an inestimable blessing when founded on right principles. Among the inalienable rights spoken of in the "Declaration of Independence" are life, liberty, and the pursuit of happiness; and who can estimate the importance of being protected in these? To bring this home to the reader let me ask, Would you have *your* brother, sister, father, mother, or child exposed to the cruelties practiced daily in Africa and other heathen lands, for any earthly consideration? Would you have them where they would be liable to be burned to death by piecemeal for the supposed crime of witchcraft, and exposed to a thousand such cruelties, and without security of life, or rights of any kind, from one hour to another, for the wealth of America?

We are largely indebted to the influence of the gospel for progress in the arts and sciences, for mechanical and agricultural enterprise, for the discovery of the power of steam, electricity, hydrostatics, and their application to a thousand useful objects. How wonderfully labor is lessened by their use, and how they add to the convenience and comfort of the people of enlightened countries, only those can fully appreciate who have resided among heathens. We are indebted to the same cause for all the refinements of society. The gospel develops and ennobles the nature of man, and greatly elevates even those who do not adopt it as a rule of action, but still enjoy its light and influence.

The influence of the gospel in our midst greatly adds to our wealth as a nation. Why is it that land in some localities in this country is worth from one to two hundred dollars per acre, while plenty of just as good land, and naturally as well located, in Africa is not worth a dime per acre? And why is it that a day's labor in this country is worth from one to ten dollars, while the same amount of labor there is worth from one to two dimes? The reason of this difference is found in the fact that we have the Bible, and they have it not. The Bible fosters invention, enterprise, and refinement wherever it goes; and wealth follows in its train.

In a very important sense the Bible has made our turnpikes, canals, and railroads, as well as the cars and boats and wagons used upon them. It has made our good houses, steam-mills, factories, ships, our trades, professions, and books. It has made our telegraph lines, by which we converse with each other thousands of miles apart. But these are the less important blessings it confers upon us. Our feeble powers are inadequate to enumerate the spiritual benefits it lavishes upon us. Take from us the Bible, and with it must go the holy Sabbath, the preaching of the sanctuary, the institutions of the church, the liberties, social, civil, and religious, which we enjoy, and *our* HOPE of heaven.

And what would be the result were we deprived of all its restraints from vice and inducements to virtue? Why, idolatry would regain its lost ascendency, superstition would stalk forth in our midst, and barbarity in its most cruel forms—such as burning persons for witchcraft, and sacrificing human beings by thousands to some imaginary deity, as is now done by some of the tribes of Africa, with an innumerable multitude of enormities such as only those can conceive who are enshrouded in the darkness of heathenism, and "led captive by the devil at his will,"—would roll upon us like a devouring flood!

We must support our home institutions, especially those which are good, and modify and make good those that are not in accordance with the Bible. If we do not sustain the institutions of Christianity in our midst it will not be two centuries until we shall be where Africa now is, in point of moral degradation, and long ere that period bloodshed and carnage will fill this pleasant land constantly.

But while we support the gospel at home, we should not fail to send it abroad. To do good, next to becoming good, is the great work of life, and if for no other reason than to ameliorate the condition of the heathen physically, we ought to give them the gospel of reconciliation. Had you a neighbor starving for want of food, and freezing for want of fuel, as a *Christian*, you would feel it your duty to alleviate his wants. Well, thousands in heathenism are now suffering daily quite as much as this man in his destitution, —we mean in a physical sense. The introduction of the gospel among them is the only remedy for their physical sufferings, as well as for their spiritual maladies; and we have the means in abundance to give them a preached as well as a written gospel. Why, we can afford to give to benevolent purposes half of all we have, and be more wealthy then than we would be to keep all we have and be without the Bible; and yet this is their sad condition.

Do not say I am speaking at random when I say that the gospel will do for the heathen what it has done for us; for physical, social, moral, intellectual and natural elevation are the legitimate results of its introduction everywhere. To have doubts as to whether it will affect the hearts and consciences of any people, when it is preached clearly, perseveringly, and in the demonstration of the Spirit, is to doubt the veracity of God's word. What God has promised he will most surely accomplish, as the history of our mission in Africa so abundantly shows, and to the consideration of which several chapters will next be given.

CHAPTER XXXVI.

LOCATION OF SHERBRO MISSION.

The first missionaries to Africa, sent there by the United Brethren in Christ, were Revs. W. J. Shuey, D. C. Kumler, and the writer, who landed in Freetown, Sierra Leone, February 26th, 1855. After remaining there a few days, they sailed down the coast about one hundred and twenty miles to Good Hope, on Sherbro Island—the name of a mission-station in charge of the American Missionary Association. This, by mutual agreement, became their temporary home, and they at once commenced prospecting the country along the Little Boom, Big Boom, Jong, and Bargroo rivers, to find a suitable place at which to open a mission. Mo Kelli, on the Jong River, being a large town, and near to a number of other towns having a large population, was thought to be a good point at one time; but it being difficult to reach, owing to the falls in the river, eleven miles below, over which canoes and boats could not pass, this project was abandoned by the missionary remaining in the field, after the other two returned to America. He next attempted to obtain a place in or near the town of Shengay, where the principal station of Sherbro Mission now is, and frequently visited Mr. Caulker, the head-man of that place, for this purpose. Receiving but little encouragement that permission would be given to commence a mission there, two trips were made up the Big Boom River, a distance of one hundred miles, to seek a location upon its banks. The last time, a selection was made; and the chiefs and head-men interested agreed to meet the missionary, to arrange terms upon which the site selected should become mission property. After waiting several days, he was compelled to abandon this project also, because the parties who alone could give the right to open the mission failed to meet as they had promised. This was late in December, and but a few days before the missionary was prostrated by his second severe attack of African fever, from which he never recovered sufficiently to do much until after he returned to America the following May. Just before leaving Africa he purchased, by the advice of the Executive Committee of the church missionary board, a mission-residence in Freetown, for the purpose of affording a comfortable place for our missionaries when there, which necessarily is more or less frequent, as that is the place at which laborers land in going to the mission, where they embark when they return, and where they receive and mail letters, do more or less trading, and frequently go for medical treatment. This would have been of great service could we have retained it; but owing to straitened circumstances, it had to be sold a few years afterward, to enable the Board to meet the current expenses of the mission.

For over six months there were no missionaries on the ground. In January, 1857, Rev. J. K. Billheimer, Dr. William B. Witt, and the writer landed in Freetown, the two former as permanent laborers and the latter for the special object of inducing, if possible, Mr. Caulker to consent to the establishment of a mission in or near the town of Shengay. Several years before, Mr. Caulker had been driven out of his town and country by his enemies in war; and he knew he could return only at the peril of his life. He finally granted permission to commence a mission near his town, more for the reason that this would give him security there than from any other consideration; and in this he realized his expectations, for soon after the mission was opened he returned to Shengay, and there was permitted to end his days in peace.

FIRST MISSION CHAPEL.

Mr. Caulker's consent was obtained in the month of March; but the rainy season being close at hand, nothing was attempted until the beginning of the dry season, about seven or eight months afterward. Pending the negotiations with Mr. Caulker the writer went to Liberia and spent near a month there, visiting the chief points of interest in that young republic, especially places along the St. Pauls River, as far as it is navigable. He fully satisfied himself that Shengay was more healthy, and in other respects preferable to it as a mission-field; and this is true of all the country he was permitted to see during the four different times he was in Africa, embracing the entire coast from Goree to Liberia. God greatly favored us in giving us so good a location. And no less marked was his goodness shown us as a church in raising up when he did the gifted, zealous, and eloquent Rev. J. C. Bright, corresponding secretary of our Board of Missions at the time the African mission was commenced, through whose untiring and effective labors the Church was aroused to engage actively in the work of missions, both at home and abroad, and who never allowed any obstacle to weaken his zeal in favor of projecting and prosecuting the mission in Africa.

CHAPTER XXXVII.

SHENGAY MISSION-STATION.

A brief description of Shengay Station, which has been and will doubtless continue to be headquarters of Sherbro Mission for years to come, with some of its surroundings, will be both interesting and profitable to all who read this book. It is a cape on the mainland, containing about one hundred and fifty acres of land, lying between the seventh and eighth degree of north latitude, and about sixty miles south from the city of Freetown. Its altitude is about twenty feet above ocean at high tide, which, with the fact that it is surrounded on three sides by salt-water, makes it quite a healthy and beautiful place. A few rods to the west of the northern point of the cape lies Williams Island, and about three miles to the north-west are the Plantain Islands, three in number, the largest having been the head-quarters of Mr. John Newton, a daring and cruel slave-trader at one time, and afterward a noted and successful minister of the gospel. The ruins of his slave-pen are still there.

The mission-land, and that occupied by the Sherbro tribe, is mostly well adapted to the growth of coffee, cotton, sugar-cane, arrow-root, ginger, rice, yams, cocoa, sweet-potato, cassada, oranges, bananas, plantains, figs, olives, cocoa-nuts, African grapes, plums, tamarinds, guava, papaws, pine-apples, sour-sop, sweet-sop, and other varieties of fruits and vegetables. There are on the mission-premises an abundance of rock and timber for building purposes, among them many palm and other valuable trees. It is altogether a desirable place, and of easy access.

The town of Shengay, where the principal chief of the Sherbro tribe resides, is but one half mile from our mission-buildings. It being the metropolis of the Sherbro country, and so near the mission, it is superior to ordinary African towns, especially the newer portions of it, where there are streets, which is quite an unusual thing in native-built towns. Near its center is Zion Chapel, a house built for the mission by Chief Caulker and his people, in which both a day and Sabbath school, as well as regular religious services, are held, the only place where these could be conducted properly, in or near Shengay, before the completion of the new stone chapel on the mission-ground two years ago. This excellent church edifice, 30 by 45 feet, with the missionary residence 32 by 40 feet in size, equally as substantial, both having stone walls and slate roofs, with several native-built houses occupied by boatmen and laborers, constitute Shengay mission-station buildings. The first building erected was a frame chapel, 24 by 30 feet, which was shipped there from New York City, all ready to be put up, in the fall of 1857. This was put upon stone pillars about seven feet high, under the supervision of Mr. Billheimer, he lodging in a native-built mudhut while it was being done. The space was divided into three apartments, one room, 20 by 24 feet in size, being used for school and meeting, and the remaining space divided into two rooms of equal size, the one for the missionary bed-room and the other for the store. The cooking was done in a native-built house close by, the hours for eating then, as now, being from 9 to 10 o'clock and from 5 to 6 o'clock; and the day-school was in session from 11 to 3 o'clock. This building was intended to be used exclusively for chapel and school-room as soon as a residence could be erected, which was commenced by Mr. Billheimer the following year; but the society not receiving the money with which to proceed, it was not finished for several years afterward. This house, put up amidst much dis-

MISSIONARY RESIDENCE.

couragement upon the part of Mr. Billheimer, is admirably adapted to the use for which it was erected, and with the kitchen and veranda since added furnishes excellent accommodations for from four to six missionaries. With care and some repairs, it will be a comfortable house for the next fifty years. The same is true of the new stone chapel. These substantial, commodious, and well-arranged buildings, with the grand scenery, both on land and the sea, make the mission-premises an exceedingly lovely spot. "Beautiful for situation, the joy of all who behold it," is Shengay Mission-Station. The patient, persevering, and self-sacrificing labors of those who gathered the material, and had it prepared and put together so as to constitute these good houses, deserve to be held in remembrance by those, both in America and Africa, in whose behalf they were built. To Mr. Billheimer belongs the honor of superintending the erection of the first chapel, and the only missionary residence we have ever had at Shengay, which he did well.

CHAPTER XXXVIII.

DR. WITT AND REV. J. A. WILLIAMS.

Dr. Witt, who accompanied Mr. Billheimer to Africa, spent most of his time at one of the stations of the Mendi missions and in Freetown, during the year and a half he remained in that country. Being well skilled in the science of medicine, a fluent preacher, and a warm-hearted Christian, he had the qualifications in a pre-eminent degree to be useful in any country, both to the bodies and souls of men, which he was to the degraded sons and daughters of Africa. At the time he received his appointment to Africa he was practicing medicine in Cincinnati, and held a professorship in one of its medical colleges. He also found time to preach frequently, and was in a pre-eminent sense a zealous doer of good works.

Mr. Billheimer having been alone at Shengay from the commencement of the work there till the beginning of the year 1859, he sought and obtained the services of Rev.

REV. WILLIAM BARTON WITT.

J. A. Williams, a native of Africa, who had been educated in one of the mission-schools in Freetown. This man rendered valuable service for over ten years. He was left in charge of the entire work a number of times, varying in length from six months to two years. But for his faithfulness and diligence in caring for the welfare of the mission, and preserving the mission-property, when the society could neither find laborers nor money to carry forward the work properly, the probability is that the buildings as well as the reputation of the mission would have been injured to such an extent as to have led to the abandonment of that work. In this and a number of other instances equally striking, the leadings of providence may be seen in a very remarkable manner.

In the month of May, 1859, Mr. Billheimer was compelled to return to America to recruit his health; and while here he did good service for Sherbro Mission, lecturing on Africa. He remained until June, 1860, when he returned to Africa; and his return was hailed with expressions of great joy by his former associates and acquaintances there. Mr. Williams was in charge of the work during his absence, and was the only laborer there. He taught the school, and kept up regular religious services most of the time with good results.

CHAPTER XXXIX.

RELIGIOUS AWAKENING, FIRST CONVERTS

For some time before Mr. Williams commenced work at the mission, and up till the time Mr. Billheimer returned to America, in the summer of 1859, there existed a religious awakening among some of the young people who attended the day and Sabbath schools, and sanctuary services. Mr. Billheimer reported a class of ten persons who were seeking the Lord, some of them very earnestly. Among the number were Miss Lucy Caulker and Mr. Thomas Tucker, who were happily converted. Thomas was a young man, twenty or more years of age. Lucy was the daughter of the chief of Shengay, and about fourteen years of age. Her parents both opposed her, and at times bitterly; but she was steadfast in her adherence to Christ. It was not long until her father sold her, to become the wife of a white man, who took her sixty miles from Shengay, to his trading-station. It is thought the old chief did this to cause her to abandon a religious life; but whether this was so or not, she continued to hold fast her profession of faith, without wavering, and does to this day. Chief Caulker himself became a Christian a few years afterward, and died. A few months after his conversion Lucy (then Mrs. Reamy) embraced the opportunity to free herself from what she regarded as an unholy alliance. She proposed to her so-called husband that they should now be married according to Christian usage or she would return to her native town, which she did while he was on a visit to his friends in England. She went to work in earnest to build her a comfortable house, which by her good management and industry was soon accomplished, and in which she lived until about one year after the death of Mr. Reamy, which took place the first of the year 1875, when she was married again. From the time she left Mr. Reamy until his death he gave her a little financial help, to enable her to educate their four children, which she was attending to well. She was an excellent Christian worker while at Shengay; and since her removal the last time she is reported as being faithful and earnest in her endeavors to lead others to accept of Christ as their Savior.

Mr. Thomas Tucker, who when he first came to the mission was an exceedingly ignorant and unpromising youth, has from the first been a devoted friend of the mission; and for some years, especially the last four or five, he has been a consistent, energetic, and influential Christian. He had severe persecution to endure and bitter opposition to overcome at the beginning of his Christian life, which thoroughly tested the genuineness of his religion. Though not without fault, he certainly has done well, and is now an exemplary Christian. His services as foreman of the mission-hands, and as captain of the mission-boat, have been very reliable. As these names, and especially Mr. Tucker's name, will be mentioned commendably several times in the succeeding pages of this book, in extracts from letters written by missionaries, nothing further will be said respecting them here.

As these two persons were the only ones who were fully brought to Christ during the first religious awakening, and the only converts in connection with Shengay Mission-Station from its commencement, in 1857, till about six or seven years ago, it may be well to inquire why there were no others. It will be remembered that at that time there were quite a number of anxious persons so far awakened as to cause them to manifest an earnest desire to know what to do to be saved; that there was but one missionary there, whose labors were frequently interrupted by sickness, and who was compelled to return to America to recruit his health soon after such religious interest was commenced. Had there been a sufficient force there to carry forward the work so well begun, doubtless there would have been quite a number brought to Christ. At different times subsequently there were excellent prospects for a glorious revival of religion, but on account of the absence of the missionary for weeks together, and sometimes of his wife also, because of his severe illness, the field so ripe for a glorious harvest of souls was not reaped. This was a source of deep regret upon the part of a number of our missionaries, and oft repeated by one of them in his letters from Africa, and frequently after he returned to America, when he often remarked, and almost with his dying breath, "Don't send any missionaries to Africa again until you are able to keep from three to four there all the time."

One thing is clearly established, namely: much was lost because we had so few laborers in Africa, and so little money to sustain them during the first fifteen years of our occupancy of that field. With but one missionary in the field, and part of the time a native helper only, much of the good done was lost. The responsibility of having so small a force there must rest with those who might have prevented it.

CHAPTER XL.

WHAT WAS DONE FROM 1860 TO 1870.

In the year 1860 Rev. Charles O. Wilson accepted an appointment to Sherbro Mission, and reached it in the month of November. After spending a short time at Shengay he returned to Freetown on business, and became seriously ill with the African fever, which kept him there for about one month, when he so far recovered as to be able to come home, which he did on the recommendation of his physician, who declared it to be necessary to save his life. This was a great disappointment, both to Mr. Wilson and the Board of Missions, and an additional discouragement to the friends of that mission. For fear that the Church would be dissatisfied with his course, and withhold money and sympathy from that work on account of his returning without rendering any service, he generously proposed to pay all the expenses of the trip, which he did.

This left Mr. Billheimer and Mr. Williams, the

native helper, alone again, which, with other discouraging features connected with the work, caused Mr. Billheimer to write the following: "Mr. Wilson is compelled to return home. We owe Mr. Heddle a large sum of money. My own health is so precarious that I shall have to leave soon; and altogether, the news to you is sad. I fear and tremble." Mr. Billheimer's health improved some, and he was enabled to remain a year after the date of this letter before coming to America.

Owing to a lack of money to meet the expenses of the mission, and our place near Shengay proving to be more healthy than was expected, there was less necessity to retain the Freetown property, and much need for the money in it. Mr. Billheimer was accordingly instructed to sell it. He soon found a purchaser; but owing to the technicalities of Sierra Leone law, and the unwillingness of some interested parties to do right, he was unable to give a good title for it. After doing all that his legal advisers suggested, he still failed to satisfy the purchasers. Early in the year 1861 he wrote home that he had done his utmost, but could not adjust the difficulty; and in a few months afterward he came to America to recruit his health, again leaving the misson in charge of Mr. Williams.

To make some disposition of this property so as

to get money, and to take care of other interests connected with the mission, the writer made a third voyage to Africa in the fall of 1861, returning the next spring. This trip cost the Church *no money*. It was attended with much peril by sea, and vexation and trial in Africa, but proved entirely successful in accomplishing the end for which it was made. The conspiracy in Freetown (for such it was) to defraud the mission of the property there, by the interposition of a kind Providence did not succeed. The property was sold, and the money obtained with which to pay most of the debts of the mission, and to make arrangements for future operations.

In the summer of 1862 Mr. Billheimer was married to Miss Amanda L. Hanby, daughter of Ex-bishop Hanby, and the following September himself and wife sailed for the field he had left the previous year. They were permitted to pursue their labors about two years, when failing health compelled them to return to America. Again the work was left in charge of Mr. Williams for nearly one and a half years. During this time several persons received and accepted appointments to go to that field, but for various reasons none of them went.

In the fall of 1866 Rev. Oliver Hadley and wife were appointed to go, and reached the mission the

REV. J. K. BILLHEIMER AND WIFE.

following December. They found the buildings in bad condition; and there was also strong opposition to our operations there upon the part of Chief Caulker and other influential citizens of Shengay, and the neighboring towns. Various reasons were assigned for this, chief of which they evidently did not mention, namely, a desire to see the mission fail. Then, too, they soon found out that the influence of Mohammedanism, purrowism, polygamists, slave-holders, and the advocates of the liquor-traffic were against them and the work they sought to accomplish. These combined, with the deep degradation of the people, constituted altogether an unfavorable state of affairs. The traffic in ardent spirits is held in high esteem there by many, and for the same reason as here, namely, the money that is in it. Slave-holders, there as elsewhere, know that when slaves become educated and enlightened they are not so easily kept in bondage. Polygamists can not see the wrong there is in one man having from two to twenty so-called wives so long as they may be used as slaves, to labor and procure for him a livelihood. Purrowism, which has exerted such a wonderful influence over the people, must continue its secret, cruel, and diabolical work; and African Mohammedans, as they can read the Arabic, and allow such abominations as slavery, polygamy, gregree-worship, and nearly all the evils prohibited in the decalogue, do not find it hard to make the people believe that their religion is as good as that of Christians. With all these things before him, Mr. Hadley saw clearly the sad condition of the heathen, and the obstacles to be removed to win them to Christ.

With a firm faith in the power of the gospel, he and his wife, who was his equal in effective evangelical labor, commenced, and continued their labors about a year and a half, when he wrote the following hopeful letter: " Our Sabbath-school is more interesting, and numbers now from twenty-five to thirty persons. Our prayer-meetings and Bible-class have been very good. Five persons whom we had hoped to see converted soon are for the present out of our reach; but another has lately given evidence of distress, on account of sin. We rejoice at every indication that the Holy Ghost is working in the dark hearts of this people."

The labors of this excellent missionary terminated at the end of two and a half years, when his rapidly-declining health compelled him to return to America in the spring of 1869. He and his wife reached their home in Indiana, April 21st, and one week afterward he died. During the few days they remained with us in Dayton, Ohio,

REV. O. HADLEY AND WIFE.

he conversed freely respecting the future of Sherbro Mission, as far as strength permitted him to do so. He knew he must die soon; and though his words were always spoken with great sincerity, yet now they were more so than usual, and possessed great unction. He insisted on keeping from three to four laborers in the field all the time; showed how much of the good that is done is lost with but one or two there, who on account of necessary absence on business, and on account of sickness, could not work to advantage. The dying testimony of this devoted Christian missionary, with the fact that he died so soon after his return to America, were regarded by some as evidence that Sherbro Mission ought to be discontinued, instead of a loud call for greater zeal and liberality in its prosecution. Several years previous, a considerable number of our people demanded its discontinuance, and now it looked as though this might be done. With a divided feeling as to what disposition to make of this mission, the question was carried to the General Conference of 1869, which, after careful investigation, advised that the door be kept wide open for its continuance, and that it be manned again as soon as men and money could be obtained to do it.

From the time Mr. Hadley and wife left Africa, in 1869, until the death of Mr. Williams in July,

1870, he had the entire charge of it again. The last two missionaries dead, and none ready to take their places, it looked as though the demand to abandon that field had become a necessity. As long as we had a trustworthy native worker on the ground we had something, but now that he is gone, and no one to take his place, we had better quit, said those who wished it discontinued. These gloomy days in the history of Sherbro Mission, and especially the fact that by the death of Mr. Williams we were without a single representative in that dark land, with its multiplied millions of deeply degraded heathen, affected others quite differently, who now had a greater zeal for the continuance of the mission than they ever had before. Among this number was one of the officers of the society, who urged the appointment of a man and his wife to go with him to Africa, which proposition resulted not in his going then, but in their being sent in November, 1870. Their names were first presented to the committee soon after the intelligence reached us that Mr. Williams was dead; but owing to the fact that the brother was not a minister, and with little evidence that they would make successful missionaries, the committee had deferred action until the month of October. This man is now an ordained minister in the United Brethren Church, and has proved to be among the most successful missionaries it has. The same is true of his wife, whose services have done much to make Sherbro Mission so highly successful during the last few years.

CHAPTER XLI.

MR. GOMER AND WIFE AND MR. EVANS SENT TO AFRICA, MRS. HADLEY'S RETURN.

Mr. Joseph Gomer and wife, whose appointment to Africa was referred to at the close of the last chapter, did not reach the mission until January, 1871, having been detained a short time in Liverpool. They found that the buildings and premises were damaged for want of attention. Mr. Williams, who had left the mission for a month or two previous to his death, to attend to some business engagements down the country, was never permitted to return to Shengay. He left the buildings and grounds in charge of a native, who paid but little attention to them.

While Mr. Gomer was discouraged at finding these things in such sad plight, he yet was greatly encouraged by a much more friendly feeling of the people to the prosecution of the mission than they had formerly shown. God had been working among the people in a marked manner without a missionary, or it may be by the death of the two who last labored in their midst. At all events, they showed a greater willingness to listen to the preaching of the gospel and a higher appreciation of its benefits than ever before. In a few months Mr. Caulker, the chief of the country, and headman of Shengay, requested that meetings be held regulary in his town as well as at the mission-house, which—owing to the destruction of our first chapel by bug-a-bugs—was now the only place on our premises in which to hold them. He attended them himself when held in Shengay, even while so feeble as to have to be carried to the place; and instead of forbidding his people, especially slaves, from being present, as he once did, he now advised, and sometimes required them to attend the meetings and the Sabbath-school. The result was, large numbers were present to hear Mr. Gomer preach, and to witness all the exercises at Bible-class and prayer-meeting. Mr. Caulker himself became a sincere inquirer after truth, and in due time an earnest penitent, as well as Christian; and he, with a number of others, publicly renounced heathenism and professed faith in Christ. Some went back to the world, but not a larger per cent than is usual under similar circumstances in America. The chief only lived a few months after his conversion, he being quite old. He died

August 15, 1871, in the faith of the gospel. His last words spoken in English were, "Salvation only through Jesus Christ, who is merciful." A few moments before his death he spoke of God, and prayed in the Sherbro language.

Mrs. Hadley, who continued to manifest much interest in the mission ever since her connection with it, now indicated her willingness to return to it, which proposal met with the hearty approval of the Executive Committee, who also appointed Rev. J. A. Evans to that field shortly afterward. They reached Shengay, December 9, 1871. Their safe arrival there was a source of much comfort to Mr. and Mrs. Gomer, who now had much more to do than they could possibly attend to properly. Equally great was the joy of Mrs. Hadley to have the privilege of meeting the people again for whom she had labored so zealously in other years, and for whose welfare she felt such deep solicitude. The following, taken from her first letter after landing at the mission, shows how she felt in view of the marked change which had taken place during her absence:

"I am thankful to God for permitting me to see the wonderful change which has taken place here since I left for America. The speaking and prayer meetings, and the Sabbath-school, are very interesting. I am encouraged to hear some bear

SHENGAY MISSION SCHOOL.

witness that the seed of other years' planting has not been entirely lost. Brother Gomer has scattered much religious truth broadcast, a good deal of which is taking root in good ground. My heart has been filled with joy and gladness while hearing these new converts speak and pray."

Ten days after she reached the mission, Mr. Gomer wrote, "There were sixty-five scholars at Sabbath-school yesterday. We have determined to build a country chapel in Shengay. Mr. Caulker—a son of the old chief who died six months previous, and his successor in office,—and his people will help do it. Our plan of operation is not yet perfected. Brother Evans and I will preach alternately here. He will keep books and accounts, and I will have charge of the laborers. Mrs. Gomer will have charge of the mission-residence, and Mrs. Hadley and Thomas Caulker will manage the school; and she will have a sewing-class."

The four missionaries found plenty to do—Messrs. Gomer and Evans giving some attention to the new chapel which was building, and Mrs. Hadley and Mrs. Gomer frequently conducting the meetings, which they did successfully. At times a remarkable religious interest pervaded all who came within the bounds of the mission. This divine influence extended to neighboring towns, and a few were induced to observe for a time some of the institutions of Christianity, such as keeping the Sabbath. Occasionally they got things so mixed as to observe Saturday or Monday in place of Sabbath, until they were set right by some one who knew the time correctly.

CHAPTER XLII.

ANOTHER CHAPEL NEEDED, APPOINTMENT OF MR. WARNER AND WIFE.

A year or two previous to this time the Executive Committee had determined to erect a new stone chapel, and appealed to the friends of Africa to forward, as a special contribution, the amount needed for this purpose. Funds for this object had accumulated until nearly enough were in the hands of the missionary treasurer, and now the chapel was needed. The one just finished in Shengay being a country-built house, would need repairs every year or two, and would only serve a temporary purpose at best. Besides, something might occur to make it impracticable to hold school and meetings in the town of Shengay, and with a permanent chapel upon the mission-premises our operations could not be interfered with. Everything indicated that the new chapel ought to be put up soon as possible.

The four missionaries already there having all that they could do, especially in view of commencing a second mission-station about fifteen miles to the south of Shengay, at which place they had been preaching as frequently as was consistent with other duties, there was a necessity for additional laborers. Accordingly, Rev. Peter Warner and wife were appointed in September, 1872, and sailed the following month. Mr. Warner's special business was to superintend the erection of the new chapel, which was the principal work he did while there. The building is 30 by 45 feet in size, and cost about $3,000, including the expense of sending Mr. Warner, and seating and painting, which was not done till the spring of 1875, when it was dedicated.

The promptness with which funds were given for this house showed that a larger number of people in the United Brethren Church were interested in the African mission than was generally supposed. The call made by the Executive Committee, asking for voluntary contributions, was published in our church papers. Contributions were sent, varying in amount from twenty-five cents to five dollars; and in a very few instances larger amounts were sent—a single congregation, or Sabbath-school, not unfrequently giving from twenty to thirty dollars. It is within the bounds of truth to say that from thirty to forty thousand people contributed money to build that house.

CHAPTER XLIII.

HOW TWO CHIEFS WHO WERE AT ENMITY BECAME RECONCILED.

Besides the wonderful work of grace at Shengay during the year 1872 another remarkable event took place near its close, which exerted a favorable influence in behalf of the mission, and gave the missionaries, especially Mr. Gomer, more power over the people than they ever had before. Mr. George Caulker, and Mr. Richard Caulker his cousin, are the principal chiefs of the Sherbro tribe; but they had been bitter enemies for about six years. This kept the country in constant unrest and trouble. Other sub-chiefs and influential head-men had taken sides in this quarrel, and hence large numbers of the people were in opposition to each other. The result was, frequent wars, and rumors of wars, and difficulties of smaller import, between the contending parties.

Mr. Lefever, a colored man, a subject of the colony of Sierra Leone, and Mr. Gomer, feeling that the cause of humanity and Christianity demanded that the unhappy strife should end, undertook to reconcile these belligerent spirits. In the face of numerous and seemingly immovable obstacles, and much delay and peril, they finally succeeded in getting them together, and to agree to bury their past differences and be friends. This was done in the presence of several hundred people, who rejoiced exceedingly, even the women clapping their hands for joy, and often thanking Messrs. Lefever and Gomer, especially the latter, whom they justly regarded as the chief instrument by which so glorious a change had been wrought.

This event favorably impressed the people in behalf of the mission, and gave Mr. Gomer great influence over them. They were now more than ever convinced that the missionaries were good men, and the mission a good institution, notwithstanding Mohammedans and others had taught them differently. This entirely destroyed the power of Mohammedanism over Richard Caulker and others who had been considerably under its influence, and who were regarded as hopeful subjects to be proselyted to that faith.

CHAPTER XLIV.

MISSIONARIES COMING FROM AND GOING TO AFRICA, INDUSTRIAL SCHOOL.

Failing health compelled Mrs. Hadley to come home in June, 1874, and in the month of November following the writer sailed for Africa, going by way of Germany for the purpose of acquainting himself more fully with the condition of our missions in both countries,—especially to make some important improvements in Africa; to organize United Brethren societies at Shengay and Bomphetook stations, and otherwise render assistance in enlarging and prosecuting our work there. This being done, he returned at the end of six months.

Mr. Gomer and wife having been there five years, they greatly needed a change; and to relieve them, Rev. J. Wolfe was appointed in August, 1875, and sailed the following October, reaching the mission in December. Mr. and Mrs. Gomer remained until April, when they sailed for America, leaving Mr. Wolfe in charge of Shengay, and Mr. Williams of Bomphetook. Mr. Gomer and wife returned in November, 1876, having been in this country six months, during which time they did much to awaken interest in behalf of our African mission, especially Mr. Gomer, by the numerous lectures delivered by him at annual conferences and other places. Meantime the Executive Committee decided to re-enforce the mission by the addition of two more laborers, to accompany Mr. Gomer and wife and to open an industrial school at Shengay,—which means to have agricultural and mechanical departments connected with the ordinary mission-work. To meet the expense of this school, a call was made for special contributions. The matter being presented to most of the conferences, the money was secured; and our people were more fully interested in the African mission than ever before. The implements needed for commencing the industrial school were bought just before Mr. Gomer and wife, Miss Beeken, and Miss Bowman sailed for Africa. These ladies were sent as teachers—Miss Beeken to be supported by the Woman's Missionary Association, which has determined to sustain a lady teacher in

Africa. This company of missionaries reached Shengay, December 21st, 1876.

With seven laborers in the field, besides native teachers, and the industrial school in operation, greater results for good are anticipated than have yet been realized.

CHAPTER XLV.

REV. J. A. EVANS.

Mr. Evans was born in Niles, Michigan, May 28th, 1848. He was converted in 1864, and united with the church of the United Brethren in Christ at Gaines, Michigan, in 1870. In October 1871 he became a member of the Michigan Conference, and was ordained to the office of an elder at the same time, and soon afterward sailed for Africa. He continued his labors in connection with Sherbro mission until August, 1873, when he returned home. The following month he was appointed to go to Virginia and labor among the freedmen, which he did acceptably for several years, and then again, by order of the Executive Committee, re-entered the service in Africa. While in Virginia he married Miss R. L. Allen, who accompanied her husband to Africa, where they expect to remain for years, life and health permitting.

Mr. Evans served as financial, or business manager, during Mr. Gomer's late visit to America. He is a good preacher, and well adapted to mission-work in Africa.

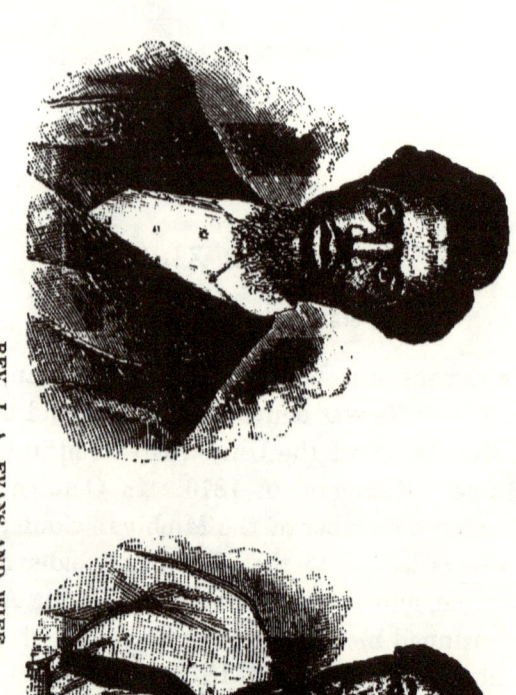

REV. J. A. EVANS AND WIFE.

CHAPTER XLVI.

EXTRACTS FROM REV. J. GOMER'S JOURNAL.

The following extracts, taken in separate paragraphs from Mr. Gomer's journal, will be found interesting as illustrating some of the phases of heathen life in Africa, the nature and strength of the superstitions which prevail, and the kind of work the missionaries have to perform:

Shortly after our arrival at Shengay, in company with Mr. and Mrs. Thomas Caulker, I went to Mocabba to visit one of our old boat-hands who was sick, and also to talk to the people. When they heard that we were come to talk to them about God they were very glad, and made preparations to hold meeting out doors. They brought seats and mats to sit upon. The old man of the town, who is said to be a very bad man, and a leader of the Purrow Society, was present and listened very attentively; and the meeting was interesting.

A great cry has been going on at Tassoh for the

death of the old king, Caulker, from the 12th of January till to-day, February 16th, and now it is to be continued at Shengay. At night they have a grand time dancing and making merry. It is a fine thing for a king to die, so that the people can make merry. But the people are fast learning better here. The blessed Bible is doing its work slowly but surely.

Going up the river for the purpose of buying lumber, we stopped for the night at a town called Mocabba. Here I made a great blunder by telling the woman who presided over the town how wrong it was to work on the Sabbath. Then I asked permission to call the people together to talk to them. She said, "she could not agree for dat," as I would tell them not to work on Sunday.

Mr. Caulker told me that he is informed that men are disguising themselves as leopards, and killing people in several villages back in the country.

On the 22d of August, 1872, the first Christian marriage that ever took place in this part of the country among natives was performed in the mission-house. Rev. J. A. Evans united together Mr. Williams and Elizabeth Caulker; also, Mr. Thomas Tucker and Miss Polly Caulker. Although the rain came down in torrents, quite a number of persons were present, who enjoyed the

REV. JOSEPH GOMER AND WIFE.

occasion much, and also the cakes and candy which came afterward.

Among the many places of interest which we visited was Fort Caulker, on Plantain Island, where Rev. John Newton spent many years of his life, first as an extensive merchant and slave-trader, then as a Christian, and an eminent minister of the gospel.

Thomas Caulker, Mrs. Hadley, Mrs. Gomer, the school children, and myself went to a town called Toombo, seven miles from Shengay. This town is the seat of government for one of Mr. Caulker's sub-chiefs, Mr. McCockle. He is head-man of the celebrated Tomo medicine. This is a native production, and its merit is said to be that it can cut a person's nose. The members of the Tomo society worship the spirits of their dead, and cook for them. They wear odd costumes, and claim to have dealings with the devil, which doubtless is true. The Tomo dance is a favorite amusement.

One Mr. Sangster came to Shengay with his daughter Yamekiah, from Tassoh. He had sold her to William Bangoora, or Soorie, one of our boatmen, for a wife, two or three months previously; but when they were to be married the mother objected to her daughter's " swearing that bad American swear." Of course they could not marry then. But the mother became sick, and finally gave her consent to the "swear." Sister Hadley, who like Dorcas is full of good works, dressed the heathen bride from her own wardrobe. Soorie was called, and Brother Evans performed the ceremony, after informing them of the nature of the oath they were about to take upon themselves.

January 9, 1873, I commenced making out the annual report of the condition of the mission. The report shows a very encouraging state of things. God has blessed our labors abundantly. The war-cloud which for many months hung over our horizon has been dispersed by Him who doeth all things well.

With Mr. Warner and wife, and Mrs. Hadley, we went on a trip up the Cockburrow River, and landed at Gendahmah. We then went up to Molacket, a town near by. Here we found a curious medicine. It is called "sengby," and is made up of a calabash, some goat-horns, small shells, old rags, and a small bell. This medicine is hung up in a pan; and powder is then placed under it, which is set on fire. Of course, the powder explodes. In their palavers the people must swear by this medicine; and they believe that if any person is guilty of perjury he will explode like the powder.

A young man is here who has for his god some leaves. He promised to bring them to me, and I am to give him a Bible in their stead.

NEW MISSION CHAPEL.

January 24, 1878. The missionaries and school-children met at the new stone chapel. Rev. Mr. Evans read portions of scripture. After singing and praying he laid the corner-stone. Next day, with my wife and Willie Caulker, I went to Bomphetook, and on the 27th we opened a school, beginning with eight scholars. We are living in a low mud-hut. Several of the people come in the evening to learn the alphabet.

Twoomah and his wife Deah came to see us, bringing with them their son, who is to attend our school; but the little fellow soon ran off. I talked with an old man who seemed quite ignorant of his Creator, and everything else. The state of ignorance to which the people are reduced is most distressing.

To-day I visited Bowmah, and asked permission to hold a meeting; but the head-woman refused. I then went to Domingo's town. He was very willing. We had a very pleasant meeting here. I also had a talk with the old chief, Bah Matty. He has a quantity of gregrees and sabbas. I tried to get them from him but failed.

We received several presents from the people. A few of them are very friendly, and kind to us, while others are bitter enemies. Especially is this true of slave-holders and polygamists who know that we oppose them in their practices. We are visited by many of the country people, who seem very anxious to look at our stereoscopic pictures, while Mrs. Gomer and I improve the opportunity to tell them of Jesus. We called on the old chief again, and while reading the Scriptures to him several came in to listen. May God bless the seed thus sown. The Shengay boys gave him a concert. He is a cripple, and can not attend service.

March 17, I visited Shengay to talk to the people. Two young men gave me their names for the seekers' class. I visited several of the converts for the purpose of encouraging them. Our Bible class is becoming very interesting, and I trust good is being done. I feel that our labor is not in vain in the Lord. There is a young man in Shengay who wishes to be a Christian; but he is a slave, and his master will not allow him to attend meeting. When Mr. George Caulker called at the mission I questioned him on the subject of slavery. He attempted to defend it, but finally admitted that it was wrong. This evening all the missionaries united in earnest prayer to God for the destruction of slavery and the spread of the gospel.

I found a great variety of medicines in Sissy's box. These were made by Murry-men. One of them is called a *thief medicine;* and they claim that the owner can steal anything without being discovered. I had them thrown into the sea.

Brother Williams and myself went to Lower Ribbe. It is a miserably dirty place. From here we went to another town called Upper Ribbe, where resides the newly-created king. This is a nice town. We were kindly received, and the people gave us good quarters. On the next morning Daddy John presented us to the king. He is a very intelligent looking man of near sixty years of age, and very dignified in appearance. He sent for all his chief men. We were very well cared for by the people, who cooked rice, fowl, cassada, fish, etc., and then met us in the barra to hear what we had to say.

The following is the prayer of an old man who lived away in the country. He had heard about God a long time ago, when Mr. Billheimer was laboring at our mission. He tried to keep the Sabbath, but he had forgotten the day on which it came. But he had one prayer, which he prayed morning and evening.

"O God, you must remember me. You must make my heart clean; make me no hate nobody; you made me; all my mind there to you. Please God, you must show me how for pray, because I don't know how."

To shoot any person is a declaration of war. If you kill with a sword or ax it is no war; but it is murder, for which the perpetrator must be burned. A fire-stick is kept stuck overhead, in the barra where they have the trial, with which they must be lighted.

Joseph T. Mason was a British subject, and a trader up the Cockburrow River, who trusted Boongamy for some rum and tobacco. After waiting several months, and Boongamy did not pay, Mason, with his laborers, went to the town where Boongamy lived, and as he was not at home they carried off all his household goods, and his daughter and her two children. Boongamy reported the affair to the king, who summoned Mason and the parties concerned to Shengay, where the palaver was talked. Both parties were required to swear on the Bible. The chief, upon hearing the evidences, decided that the children must be held as security until the debt was paid. The children were left at Shengay for safe keeping, while Boongamy and Mason returned to their homes—Boongamy to raise rice and make palm-oil to redeem his grandchildren from slavery, and Mason to sell rum and tobacco, and spread misery through the country. Meantime the children were put into school at Shengay and were learning fast, both to read and sing. Little Mary Ann Boongamy was a very interesting child of about six or seven years of age; but alas! fate was against her. Her grandfather soon took sick and died. The people said that bad swear that he swore on the Bible, that white man swear, had caught and killed him. Poor little Mary Ann was sold or traded to the Soosoo people for a cow. Oh, how very sad we felt when we heard of it.

Piomi is chief of the Turtle Islands. Although these islands—twelve or fifteen in number—belong to the British, they allow the natives to manage their own affairs, religiously and politically, as there is not enough trade here to make it profitable to keep a government official. Piomi is a man between fifty and sixty years of age. In 1871 he came over to Shengay on a visit, and to see a girl that had been given him for a wife when she was yet a child. She was given him by the old king; but she was left with her mother until she was old enough to become his wife, so he returned to his home to wait two years longer. Missionaries were now in Shengay. Susannah—for that was the girl's Christian name—became interested on the subject of religion. Mrs. Hadley, one of the missionaries, took a great interest in her. She obtained pardon and was happy in her Savior's love. But time flew, and the old heathen chief, who already had a great number of wives, came for his young bride. This was a sore trial to poor Susannah, for she had no love for the old man;

and then there were no missionaries on the islands, and she would be among the lowest of heathens. She protested against going, and begged her mother to save her. This her mother could not do, as the old king had given her to this man; and now that the king was dead they must respect his acts. The poor girl came to the mission, crying as though her heart would break, to tell the missionaries good-by. After committing her to God in prayer, Mrs. Hadley gave her a Bible and she left for her new home. Here she led a wretched life, as the other wives did. She had been there about a year when the missionaries went over to one of the islands. Susannah soon heard that the missionaries had come, and crossing the island upon which she lived, on foot, she came by canoe to see the missionaries. Her meeting with Mrs. Hadley will not soon be forgotten. Next day she brought one of her sister-wives with her, also the Bible given her by Mrs. Hadley, and desired that she should read to them. Her husband, if he may be called such, told us that ofttimes she would take this Bible upon her lap and sit for a long time crying, and would say that her good friend had given it to her. Some months after this Susannah got sick, and the old chief sent her to her mother. She soon recovered, and was again attending meetings in Shengay. Her husband came for her, and again the mother tried to save her; but the king said she must go. They went fifteen miles down the coast to take a boat. Here she met one of her brothers, who was a convert. He took her from the old chief and brought her back to Shengay; but the old chief recaptured her and took her back. Shortly after, he was arrested by the British government on suspicion of dealing in slaves, and sent to Freetown and there confined in jail; and while there, Susannah made good her escape and went with her mother to the Bomphe country, where Piomi can not get her. While with her husband she received no support from him whatever, but had to feed and clothe herself as best she could.

Many native Africans, in their heathen state, are given to thieving on a small scale. Especially do they steal something to eat whenever they can find it, unless it is protected or watched over by what they call medicine. There is a great variety of this medicine. It is frequently made by Murrymen, or country-fashion men, as they are called. The Murry-men are Mohammedans, who write in Arabic. They write sentences of the Koran and do it up in different forms, either in horns, in calabashes, or in shells, and sometimes in cloth. A little hut is built, usually at the entrance of the farm, and the medicine is put there in a conspicuous place, so as to be seen by all. It is claimed that whoever steals anything from this farm, the medicine would catch him; he would get bad sickness. The country-fashion men get stones, shells, bug-a-bug hills, and many other foolish things, and set them up as medicines, to watch farms. Very few natives would dare steal where they see any of the above named medicines. Our converts are not allowed to put any kind of medicines on their farms, and frequently they suffer severely from theft. The thieves seem to search for the farms of the God people, as they call Christians, knowing that they do not put medicines on their farms. The Murry or medicine men also have smooth boards; and if any one is sick they write, with a piece of chalk, passages of the Koran. They then wash it off in a bowl of water and give the water to the patient to drink. I once saw a Murry-man give a patient this water to drink. The patient died. I said to the Murry-man, "Daddy, your medicine no use." He replied, "Medicine use, but that daddy head too stronger;" that is, the man had no faith in the medicine, and hence died.

Mr. Reamy, Lucy Caulker's husband, was an Englishman, and an agent for an English trading-house on York Island. A native from the country got in debt to him, and having nothing to pay he gave his son in pawn for security. He turned the boy over to Lucy, and afterward went to England for his health. Lucy moved to Shengay, and took the boy, whom she called John, with her. Here she might have held him as her slave if she chose. But instead of doing this she sought work for him, and encouraged him to buy clothes and books and learn to read. He became a regular attendant at the Sabbath-school. He is now twenty years old, and concluded that he would like Chooca, a young girl who is living with Mr. Williams, at Bomphetook, for a wife; but her parents were not willing for her to be married like white folks. Next, Lucy tries to get Karry Myalis' daughter. John says "he likes the girl, and the girl likes him, but her father and mother will not consent for their daughter to marry white-folks' fashion; and furthermore, the missionaries have spoiled his medicines, that he had to mind his farms." But Lucy persevered, and found another girl for John, whose parents agreed that she might marry Christian fashion. John is very industrious, and is working hard to earn money to build him a house in which to live.

CHAPTER XLVII

LETTERS WRITTEN BY MISSIONARIES.

The following extracts from published letters written by missionaries while in Africa during the last four years are interesting and instructive. They will appear in the order in which they were written as to time, accompanied with the name of the writer, except those written by the author of this volume.

WORK IN A HEALTHY CONDITION.

I am happy to say that the work here and at Bomphetook is in a very healthy state, and we thank God for the prospect. John Caulker, the Mohammedan, who has done much harm to the work, got himself into trouble. Mr. Caulker called all the chief men together at Shengay, and John was arraigned on many charges, preferred against him by Mr. Caulker, the chief, which were proved. Among the charges was one of trying to hinder the spread of the gospel, the only thing

calculated to elevate the country. He told the
story of the king of Abyssinia sending to Queen
Victoria to know what made her country so great,
and how she sent him a copy of the Bible. The
missionaries are here to teach us. They are our
friends. If you want to drive any one from the
country (John had tried to have the people at
Shengay and Bomphetook drive the missionaries
from the country, saying they were spoiling it), let
it be the traders, who are spoiling the country with
rum and tobacco. We don't need their rum or
tobacco. The chief has been very friendly of late,
sending us presents of fruit and vegetables from
his garden. A few weeks ago a child died in
Shengay. He had her taken to the chapel, called
all the school-children, and as many adults as
would come, and delivered an address to them on
the certainty of death and the blessings of the
gospel; admonishing all to prepare for death.

JOSEPH GOMER.

PURROW, TOOMAH, BUNDOO, AND YASSA.

On the 24th of January, 1875, Mr. Gomer and
myself were at Bomphetook. At 6 o'clock A. M.
we had prayer and class-meetings, at 11 o'clock I
preached, at 2 o'clock P. M. Sabbath-school, and at
7 o'clock Mr. Gomer preached. All these meetings were poorly attended. Upon making inquiry

as to the reason why, the reply was, "The Bundoo Society done met close by last week, and the people, especially women, go there."

The Bundoo is a women's secret society, and at this time was in session within six or eight miles of Bomphetook, and had created a good deal of excitement among the people in all the towns, some five or six in number, between Shengay and Bomphetook. The particular event which produced this was the fact that one of Chief Caulker's girls, and one or more of the girls of each head-man in all these towns, had run away to join the Bundoo. Our chief's head-wife, and the head-wife of another town close to Bomphetook, were after their runaway daughters on this day. Chief George Caulker, and his father before him, with other head-men in the Sherbro country, are opposed to all these secret societies, and this explains why their daughters ran away to join the Bundoo, and why the mothers of these girls were after them to prevent them from uniting with the society.

All we have been able to learn of the Bundoo is, that it is among the women about the same that the Purrow is among men. Both practice circumcision, and are institutions having some age, and exerting considerable influence. Especially is this true of the Purrow Society.

The Purrow and Toomah are composed of men

exclusively, and the Bundoo and Yassa of women. The Toomah and Yassa are of recent origin.

Rev. B. Root, an educated native of that country, stated to the writer the following in regard to the Purrow Society:

"It exerts a wonderful influence over the civil and religious institutions of that country. The three particular things it teaches are, resolution, reticence, and endurance; and it is composed mostly of freemen, and the better or smarter members of society. The chiefs are generally Purrow-men, and the society controls them and indicates the policy they must pursue in most matters of importance. There are but three degrees, two of which are not regarded as very important, but the third is all-important and binding. When the Purrow decides a matter, it is as though the Supreme Court did so in our country. It is the highest authority known; and woe to the man who goes contrary to its requirements.

"This society impresses the uninitiated and lower classes with a fear which is remarkable, and makes them easy victims to any oppression or injustice which it may impose upon them; and yet it often conserves the peace and purity of society, and especially of its own members. There are times when to use an impure word is a punishable offense, and those who do it are made to feel the power of the Purrow. It is of great antiquity, coming to the west coast of Africa from Egypt."

That it puts out of the way, by assassination, objectionable chiefs and head-men there is no doubt,—sometimes by a party of men going out and murdering outright, or by administering poison through persons who are regarded as fast friends of the party to be disposed of. It is, in short, a powerful organization, and one which, like slavery and polygamy, will require time to destroy. It stole one of our first converts, and carried him away and concealed him, at two different times, and the last time, by force, made him a Purrow-man, and put him through a severe drill. He finally saw a way of escape, and left the Purrow-ground, a dense thicket, and came back to the mission, where he still remains.

DEDICATION OF A CHAPEL AT BOMPHETOOK.

Brother Flickinger dedicated the first house of prayer in this, one of the strongest citadels of the devil, within one hundred yards of the great Purrow-bush, last Sunday, the 28th of March. It was a most interesting and refreshing occasion. The congregation was unusually large. All the benches were filled, and others had to be brought in from the neighboring huts. The text was, "My house shall be called the house of prayer." The chief, George S. Caulker, interpreted. The congregation then stood up while I read a part of Solomon's dedicatory prayer, which was also ably interpreted by the chief, sentence after sentence. At the close of the reading Brother Flickinger offered the dedicatory prayer. The Sabbath-school scholars then chanted the one hundred and thirty-sixth psalm.

After this I baptized three persons, and we administered the Lord's-supper to eleven individuals. Evidently the Lord was with us. It was a time never to be forgotten by any who were present. Though the service was unusually long, yet none seemed tired. There were absent, from unavoidable causes, three candidates for baptism and seven for church-membership.

At the close of the Sunday-school in the afternoon, a church, composed of eight members, was organized.

The house is 30 by 20 feet, and capable of comfortably seating one hundred and twenty people. It will cost about £20 when quite completed and inclosed.   J. M. WILLIAMS.

WHAT THINGS COST IN AFRICA.

To support a mission in western Africa costs materially For instance, we paid five dollars per hundred for lumber in Freetown, and on the ground here it cost seven dollars per hundred. Missionaries must have lumber to build houses in which to live, teach, and preach. We also bought native lumber, which is quite irregular in thickness, and green, for four dollars and a half. We paid thirty-six cents for a lamp-chimney, worth eight or ten cents; and everything in the furniture line is very costly here.

Missionaries must have boats. To keep the boats and buildings in repair is a constant bill of expense; and to run a boat, five or six men are needed, who cost, in this country, from six to eight dollars a month.

The cement sent here to fix the bank cost in New York a dollar and sixty cents per barrel; to bring it to Freetown cost two dollars and fifty cents, and from Freetown to Shengay one dollar. Then to get it from the vessel to the schooner, and from the schooner ashore, cost about forty cents more per barrel. Some extra charges were made for cooperage, etc., so that it cost here about six dollars per barrel.

Mr. Gomer took his sick wife to Freetown to obtain medical attention. He rented a house for thirteen dollars a month. In less than a week the doctor told him he must take his wife to Regent, a mountain-town five miles away, if she was to be benefited. To make her comfortable, he must rent a house there at ten dollars a month, but a whole month's rent must be paid for the first house; so you see he paid twenty-three dollars house-rent for that month. Then it cost five dollars to get his wife and things to Regent; then he had to hire a cook and nurse at six dollars a month, and the doctor's bill was ten pounds and thirteen shillings, or over fifty dollars. The entire cost of this trip was not less than one hundred and fifty dollars during the two months that she was away; yet this outlay of money could not be avoided.

Many things seem cheap here, as labor, for instance, but still they are much dearer than in the United States. We pay our carpenters and masons from twelve to fifteen dollars, and the common laborers from six to eight dollars a month; but one good mechanic in America will do as much as four or five of these, and so of the laborers. Then you must be with them here much of the time, showing them how to do the work, and when it is done, you feel sad to think that both they and yourself had so little sense.

Not less than five hundred dollars are annually required for repairs, to keep the mission-residence and the chapels and boats in good condition. Then, to keep four missionaries, with the school-teachers necessary, and the common laborers for manning boats and doing other necessary work, will require at least three thousand more. In case of much sickness, or having to go abroad in search of health, from four to five thousand dollars are needed every year.

NUDE AFRICANS.

On my return from Shengay to America I spent several days in Freetown, awaiting a vessel in which to sail. There is a great deal of living out-doors. The weather is always warm, and during one half the year there is no rain; and many of the people are quite indifferent as to whether they are in or out of doors, as well as to whether they are in or out of clothing. Their habits of going naked there, especially boys and girls until they are ten or twelve years old, outrages one's sense of propriety. But this is common all along the west coast of Africa. To put a stop to naked boys and girls coming to the mission-house, they had to be punished. We publicly and privately preached the gospel of dress, and showed the people that their licentious practices could never be corrected until they dressed. Nakedness is a crime against humanity, and contrary to the law of God, and should be punished severely. The great curse of Africa,—that which causes more converts to backslide than all other evils,--is licentiousness; and nakedness conduces much to it.

DEDICATION OF THE CHAPEL AT SHENGAY.

"Thanks be to God which giveth us the victory." We are organized at last, and our beautiful new chapel is dedicated to God. We have labored under great disadvantages, many of our people being away. The whole country is in a state of excitement. One John Caulker has a party of Kossoo warriors, who are committing serious depredations in the country, in consequence of which it is in a state of confusion. On the 3d, 4th, and 5th of April three villages were plundered by the robbers.

On April 2d we met a few of our members in the country chapel at Shengay. Mr. Flickinger told them that we intended to organize a church on the following Sabbath, and stated what would be required of those who united with us, namely, that no one owning slaves, or who is a member of the Purrow Society, or a polygamist, or who sells or drinks intoxicating liquors as a beverage, could be a member of our church. On the morning of the 4th the chapel was pretty well filled. Mr. Flickinger preached, taking for his text Psalm xxvii. 4, and after the sermon Rev. J. M. Williams, of

Bomphetook, read the seventh chapter of II. Chronicles. Next the dedicatory prayer was offered. A class of sixteen members was organized. Others had given me their names to unite with us, but because of sickness, and for various other reasons, they were not present. At 7 o'clock in the evening the new chapel was brilliantly lighted by the new lamps that were donated by the Hicksville Sabbath-school. Many thanks to those dear friends of poor, degraded Africa. Rev J. M. Williams delivered a very pointed and practical discourse from Matthew xxvii. 23, after which twenty-seven partook of the sacrament.

A few words about the new chapel before I close, it is plastered inside and out, and has had the walls strenghtened with iron rods. The woodwork is all painted nicely; and good, substantial seats, that will comfortably seat two hundred and twenty persons have been provided. Thanks be to God who put it into the hearts of those good people in America to build a house for God here in this dark land.

JOSEPH GOMER.

Shengay, West Africa, April 6, 1875.

SUICIDE BY AN AFRICAN.

I have received five members since you left, one month ago. Our meetings and Sabbath-schools are good, and the Bible-class is very large. A man came to me, a few days ago, and professed to have been converted, gave a very good experience, and wished to join the Church; but he had two wives. "One of them had had four children by him, but she hold no God-palaver; the other one hold God-palaver long time, but she no have any children." Now which one can be left so he can join the Church. He says he must join; but this is a difficult matter to settle.

The chief is doing well. He has sent three men to Bomphetook to assist Brother Williams with his house. Yesterday we received word that one of the villages which John Caulker's men had plundered was bringing a war party to Shengay. David's father had a palaver at Bomphetook on last Sabbath. Brother Williams happened in at the chief's house when they were talking. He told them that if God sent trouble upon them very soon, they would know what it was for. Before the morning meeting was over a cry was heard, and, on inquiring the cause of it, it was found that one of the chief's children had been drowned in the sea. Afterward, Cosambo, David's father, loaded his gun heavily, put the muzzle in his mouth, and blew his brains out. The palaver had gone against him. The people said he had "some bad thing in him, what made him do so; maybe witch live there;" and they cut him open to see, but found no witch. Thus you see how the devil is working, and we must be up and doing.

JOSEPH GOMER.

Shengay, West Africa, May 17, 1875.

GODS DELIVERED TO MISSIONARIES.

We have great cause to be thankful for the permanency of the sea-wall and the church. I claim success for both. I thank God that in the spiritual work we have nothing to complain of. The leaven is working. Our Bible class is well attended by both old and young, who seem to take a deep interest. I received six into the Church lately, and dropped one. There are many of the poor slaves that would unite but for the proud Pharisees who stand in the door. But we are praying; and God hears prayers. Our meetings are good. Taosoh, Shooney, and Cattah, are now having preaching every Sabbath. They give us a house at the two former places, and at Cattah they have built a very small barra. We shall add Tissannah as soon as the rains slack a little.

The children are all improving rapidly in writing, arithmetic, and grammar.

I spent a Sabbath at Bomphetook, a few weeks ago, but the rains were very heavy, and few people came out. However, it is very evident we are gaining ground there. Mr. Cole, the teacher, gave me a large mangro god that he got from Contam, the chief's mouth-piece, and he now sends his boy to school. Rev. Mr. Williams brought me another large wooden god, which the owner had got tired of.

I saw the governor in town. He says he thinks Shengay will be annexed to British Sherbro.

Lucy Caulker is a great help to us in our work; and she deserves great credit for her zeal in putting down evil and standing up boldly for Christ. Mrs. Neal has a class of adults, and is doing well in the Sabbath-school. Lucy and Betty Caulker take the infant class, numbering from thirty to forty, and teach them scripture lessons and to sing. You see, native help is already doing considerable. God is for us, and we are on the winning side.

After having gone to bed last night, some man came from Tassoh in great haste for the mission-boat—a canoe having been upset at sea, and one man was already drowned, and another was clinging to the canoe. It was the time of high water, and a gale had been blowing for several days. I let the boat go, and our captain with it; but they were too late to save the man. This man had often attended our meetings, but had never made a profession of faith in Christ. There are thousands in this country driven by the devil out in the great ocean of sin. The storm has been raging for many years, and many precious souls have dropped

unprepared into eternity because the gospel ship was not there to rescue them. The cry comes from villages about us, "Bring us the gospel; we are sinking; we are perishing; we are swamped in this ocean of sin; bring us the Bible. We want a safe religion—a religion with which we can feel secure. These charms, these gregrees, these sabbas, these wooden and stone gods, these bug-a-bug hills are not able to save us. The sea is rough. We want, we must have, the gospel ship. Bring it to us." But precious souls, redeemed by the blood of Christ, must perish, because our numbers are too small! JOSEPH GOMER.
Shengay Mission-house, July 20, 1875.

YESTERDAY A BLESSED DAY.

Yesterday was a blessed day—a day of such joy that we wept for gladness. The cause is that it can now be said of our head-man Bah Matty, "Behold, he prayeth." Our Jesus is the conqueror. Satan's kingdom is already shaking at Shengay and Bomphetook. Yesterday afternoon Bah Matty sent to ask us to come and pray for him in his house. Joyfully we accepted his offer. After the regular evening service, a large number accompanied us to the chief's house. Again I spoke briefly to him. Nearly all the prayers were offered by our native brethren and sisters. The chief wept like a child. Finally, he fell on his knees and cried, "O Ogbatukeh" (O God), and continued praying, while we all bowed too. Some wept, while others, who understood the burden of his petition, loudly said, "Konay, Ogbatukeh" (Do, God). Another has cried to God, also. The last two Sabbaths our congregation has been unusually large. Among those added to our regular hearers is Kong Tom, the next man to Bah Matty in Bomphetook. A few months ago he was so enraged that he threatened to bring myself and "Daddy" Williams to their "barra," or court of justice, for erecting the barra without order from the chief. He did all he could to oppose the work. Now, when at home, he is both a regular and attentive hearer of the word. He is now a good friend of ours. Two interesting youths from Kai and a woman were added to the number of believers in the Lord. Two others were baptized, and three were added to the Church. At a church meeting held June 23d it was agreed that this chapel be named Otterbein.

J. M. WILLIAMS.

TRIP UP THE BOMPHE RIVER.

Thomas Caulker, Thomas Tucker, and myself started on a trip up the Bomphe River, for the purpose of preaching and to buy some rice. We touched at Mammoo, and slept at Conollo. Next morning we passed on to the town of Bomphe. Here we found King Richard. The king says if we will furnish a school-teacher, he will give us the grounds and put up a country-house for school and dwelling. From here we passed on to Pho-Phi, and Candobee, a few miles further up the river. As we entered the town we were met by a very old woman, who ran to meet me, clasped my hand in both of hers, then danced and capered about like a child. When this first outburst of joy was over, she told me that " before time when Mr. Billheimer been in the mission she been live there and cook for them boatmen, and that time she been hear 'bout God, but she no been hear good, for she no been go inside the meeting; she been shame; she want to go back to the mission again, but she done loss all her teeth." When we told her that we were going to keep a meeting there that night, she took another dance. There is a small barra here, where the Mohammedans pray and teach some children to read and write Arabic. We got permission to occupy this barra, and soon all the people in town were assembled at the meeting. I never saw better attention paid anywhere. Early next morning I heard a man crying at the top of his voice something in the Timiny language; and he was walking all through the town, hallooing as he went in a very angry manner. On inquiring, I learned that some one had stolen a fowl from him, and he was publishing to the town that if this was repeated he would go and swear "on one bad medicine, and if any one steal from him again bad sickness must catch them, and swell their belly, and all their bones must hurt um so they can't sleep; sores must come all over their skin, and bad sick must eat their noses; and that some sick must come on all their family; and whoever sorry for them must get all same sick."

From here we went to a new town not named yet, as there were but few people in it. Our stay was short. About 4:00 P. M. on the 8th we landed at Gondohoe, and walked to Senehoe, a short mile. In population it would make four of Shengay. The people are mostly Mendis, with a few Timinies, and a sprinkle of Sherbros. This is where the chief, Banyah, or Hanyah, resides. He was not at home, however. The chief is a raw heathen; and they say he has one hundred and eighty wives. He is not an old man, and has more power over his people than any other king in the country. He furnished many soldiers for the Ashantee war. I talked to them from John i. 12, 13. A young man from Freetown who knows book tried to interpret in Mendi, but my English was too strong, as they say; so Mr. Parker, who interprets for the chief, did it. J. GOMER.

September 6, 1875.

EVILS OF THE LIQUOR TRAFFIC IN AFRICA.

To say that liquor kills more than the sword is putting it very weak. It not only kills more, but worse; for the sword only kills the body, but this kills pockets, reputation, mind, soul, and body, and not unfrequently wife and children. It is more to be dreaded than small-pox, or cholera, or any known epidemic. It is the concentration of everything that is degrading and ruinous. No kind of devilish, low business can well get along without it. It is the scourge of all Christian and heathen lands. Having made four trips to Africa, the cargo upon each vessel, with one exception, was principally rum. Rum and missionaries—but hundreds of barrels of rum to one missionary—go to heathen lands. In western Africa it is the curse of curses now. In other days it did much to carry on the slave-trade. One barrel of rum has been known to purchase quite a number of slaves; and often by getting the people drunk slave-traders carried them away without giving any remuneration, which was indeed but little worse than to get them by giving the rum to head-men, who would make war upon some small unprotected town and steal them and deliver them to the slave-merchants. Going there I encountered several severe gales and storms, and a few times was in danger of being lost at sea; but the greatest danger I ever encountered was on account of a drunken captain.

I was in a town in Africa, where it was told that a drunken head-man had a man beheaded for picking up two or three of his palm-nuts and eating them! The poor fellow had lost himself the morning before, and wandered about most of the day and all night without anything to eat, and found his way home early in the morning. Passing by the head-man's palm-nuts, he picked up and ate a couple, but was reported to the head-man, who ordered him killed outright, and it was done. This head-man had not yet sobered up fully from his drunk the day before on American rum.

Among the first things I saw in Africa when landing there, twenty-two years ago, was a number of barrels of rum from a whisky-rectifying establishment in Cincinnati, Ohio. Some Christian farmers had raised the corn, it may be, that made that rum. Could they, and all lovers of good morals and religion, know the evils of the liquor traffic in Africa, they would not only not sell grain to make it, but would labor to put down the traffic.

WORK AT BOMPHETOOK.

The sudden outbreak of war not only stopped me from itinerating, but threatened to suspend our work at this station. Bomphetook and surrounding towns were depopulated by the flight of their inhabitants before the enemy. Bah Matty and other chiefs fled over to British Sherbro. This greatly affected our congregations and schools, and that just when there was a necessity to add to our benches to accommodate the increasing number of the congregation.

Bah Matty and many of the people returned from their hiding-places last Friday and Saturday. Myself and Brother Wolfe called on him on Sunday morning. On my asking him, "What news?" he said, "No news; only I done send word, and the people are washing themselves to get ready to go to pray." At the eleven o'clock service the barra was more crowded than ever. All the benches in the neighborhood, besides those we have, were insufficient to contain the people who came out to worship the Lord our God. At our last quarterly meeting two persons were added to the Church.

Mrs. Williams commenced a children's weekly prayer-meeting soon after her return to the station. It is held in the barra every Friday evening. It is very interesting and encouraging to hear the heathen children speaking to God and praying in the name of Jesus. We feel it our duty to labor all we can and pray more for success among the young. We begin to see signs of spiritual life among the children. God be praised. The number of members on the list since our organization is twenty-one; removals to other parts of the country, three; dismissed from membership, four. The number on the list of the inquirers' class during the year 1875, not admitted into the Church, was twenty-two; removed and carried away to the interior, fifteen; number in attendance, six; under the watch-care of the Church, one. The number on the day-school list is twenty-five.

A Yassa dance was got up and kept Bomphetook noisy for a week, by an elderly woman, just at the time I expected a favorable result. The Purrow devil was out twice, the destruction of the cassada farms by wild hogs and of several lives by sharks being believed to be the work of human beings transformed to wild hogs and sharks. I lost no opportunity for several weeks, in public and private, to battle against such heathenish beliefs, and to show that these, with the unsettled state of the country, were the voice of God to their chiefs and people. Just when signs of success began to show themselves, a "country doctor," or "medicine-man," from the Mperreh country visited Bomphetook, and called upon the people and surrounding chiefs to "make the devil-heart lie down," that he may drive away all bad from the country, and prove (expose the individuals who were transforming themselves into) the wild hogs and sharks. This fetich-man sold a great quantity of his medicines, and on the 21st ultimo he called a general meeting, which I attended with Mr. Cole, with our Bibles. We found this deceiver bowing down in a state of perfect nudity, the people standing around, while he spoke to a stone on which was spilled the blood of several white fowls, and to which was offered rice boiled with palm-oil and the fowls.

The chief of Sammah is among those who are persuaded to pray in the name of Jesus. The chief of Compah called himself to see me, and begged that I would call again to speak to them the word of God. J. M. WILLIAMS.

October 1, 1875.

WAR PARTY ON BARGROO.

I thank God that we are still in good health, and that no war has disturbed us here. As soon as the Ramadan Fast was over, contrary to expectation, the war party made a raid into British Bargroo, near Mr. Burton's saw-mill. Several towns were plundered and many people carried off—among them one of Mr. Burton's sawyers and the husband of his school-mistress. Mr. Davis, the commander at Bonth, mustered his police force and went to the war barricade and demanded the prisoners. They would not open the barricade. Mr. Davis ordered his men to cut through it. He was shot through the neck, hand, and in the breast, and four policemen were killed on the spot. Davis' men retreated, carrying him away badly wounded. The Kossoos, it is said, now killed all their Sierra Leone prisoners, among them Mr. Burton's sawyer. They then evacuated the barricade and started for the Kossoo country. In their hasty march they threw away their baby prisoners in the bushes. One was picked up alive, and others were found dead. Word was immediately sent to the governor, who took eighty soldiers, and I believe about sixty policemen, and went to Bonth.

I landed at Freetown on the night of December 13th, and found Brother Wolfe there. We are preparing to start for Shengay on the 16th. Smallpox is still raging in and about Shengay and Bomphetook. The governor has caught John Caulker. Commander Davis is improving.

On the 22d I sent Tom up the Cockburrow for some rice. He landed at one of the towns not yet plundered, but it was full of Kossoo warriors. A number of the Kossoos were there, and seized the boat before it had fairly landed. One, in attempting to take the rudder from Tom, got worsted; for Tom clinched him; and Tom says, "I show him someting." It so happened that there was a big head-man in the town who was a good friend to the mission. He knew Tom and the mission-boat. He interfered and all was restored again. They gave him two men to guard him and his rice while he was there. The same day Brother Williams came from Bomphetook. We went up the river to Tom.

On the 11th the plundering commenced, and was kept up, at intervals, until the 24th. I have not felt any fears that they would trouble us at the mission. We will do all in our power to protect the property, and leave the rest with God. The people are saying, already: "Look how God great; he stop dem Kossoos from plunder Bomphetook and Shengay." JOSEPH GOMER.

November, 1875.

THEY HAD NEVER SEEN GOD.

It was 6 o'clock in the evening, January 31st, 1876, when Rev. A. Menzies and myself shoved out in the little mission-boat Sandusky for Seneho, at the head of the Bomphe River. By 10 o'clock we were in the river, and by 2:00 A. M. we were at Condobee, where there is a large trading-establishment belonging to a Mr. Zizer. It sits high up on a side hill. The night was dark, but the faithful watchman had a bright fire burning to warn off wild animals, sneak-thieves, and war-parties. He met us at the wharf. "Is Mr. Zizer at home?" I asked. "No," said the watchman; "he go one town, but he come to-morrow." "Well, tell Mr. Brown, the clerk, strangers come to see him." "He no deh; he done go he country." "Is Mrs. Zizer here?" "No." "Well, open the house, then; we wish to sleep here until morning. Our boat is too small to sleep in, and the dew is heavy." "Wait first," said he; and wait we did, about five minutes, when he returned with Mr. Zizer, who gave us a hearty welcome.

Seneho is at the head of navigation on the Bomphe River. We wish to go to Tyami, a large town in the Mendi country. But we can not pass through a town without the chief's consent. He is not at home, but is sent for. Toward evening his head-man comes, bringing a duck as a present from the chief, who says we must wait for him; he is coming just now. So we have to wait. Mr. Parker, the head-man, gives us a large board house to stay in, in which we hold a meeting at night. Next morning the chief was still absent. We waited until 3:30 P. M., when we left.

At 7:30 p. m. we reached Yeauyeamah, about twelve miles from Seneho. Here we found the king of Tyami and several of his chiefs. They were met together here to consult each other and devise the best means for catching one Karrybahum, who had assisted in plundering some towns in British Sherbro. The English governor had demanded him of these chiefs, as he was hiding in their territory. These chiefs were also trying to get their people together in order that they might collect from them ten thousand bushels of rice—a fine put upon them by the governor. When we landed the news spread that the governor had come again, and many of the people ran away. The chiefs said they could not let us go to Tyami, as we had already spoiled their work.

In answer to a question if they know anything about God, they said they had never seen him, as he had never been to their town, but if he would come there they would be glad.

We must go back; and when this palaver is done they will send us word, and we may go to Tyami—but not now, because the people would become frightened at us. JOSEPH GOMER.
February, 1876.

"BIG-BIG WITCH-BIRD."

I had a long talk with Sateah-Kate about her

children. She had recently left Martin, a village up the Mamboo River, where she said a "big-big witch-bird eat all her pikins" (babies). Two of them had recently died, and she believed that a large bird which lived in the bush and made a strange noise had caused the death of her children; and she would not go to live there again. I tried to show her that these birds have no power over people. I told her that I believed God was very angry with her because she tied charms and gregrees on her children, and when they were sick trusted in them and in the country-fashion man to cure them; so God took them. She says that I have got a big devil, and turn the people's heads. She will not believe what I tell her. I return to the mission. I see a sail far out at sea. It heads toward the mission. It is the church missionary boat, and Rev. Mr. Menzies is in it.

Next morning, with Thomas Caulker, and four school-boys to sing, we go by way of the sandy beach to Tassah. I look into the huts to say goodmorning. In one a man is lying on a mat spread on the ground. His face and body are smeared all over with clay. On inquiring the cause, he said "he yet yanger sick." "Yanger" means gentry, or genteel. The natives will not speak the word "small-pox,"—that was what ailed him. They must speak well of the disease, and call it by nice names. A woman in one hut is sitting on a mat by the fire, her body, limbs, and face covered with sores. She would come to meeting, but "sick won't let her." She wants us to give her some tobacco. We hold a short meeting; there are only nineteen present besides our own party. We go to Shooney. The tide is up, and we have to cross a creek, one at a time, in a very small paddle-canoe. The boys swim. After meeting, one man wants to see me privately in his hut. He gets his god, gives it to me, and says: "Take um; I no want um again." It was the tooth of some large animal, perhaps a hippopotamus. From here we went to Cattah. Here Daniel Party, one of our former school-boys, has built for us a small barra. At the former places our meetings were in the open air. By 10:00 A. M. we are all back to the mission, having held three meetings.

JOSEPH GOMER.

March, 1876.

"GOD DONE TAKE THE COUNTRY."

With the beginning of the year it seemed as though Satan had awakened out of a sleep, shook himself, and set to work in earnest, putting forth every effort in his power to hinder the progress of the gospel in this field of labor. He selected for his prime agent John Caulker, a Mohammedan. It would have been very difficult for him to choose a more energetic or daring person. But, thanks be to God, he has given us the victory. John Caulker and his accomplices are to-day in Freetown jail, and all his efforts to put out the fire which the gospel has kindled have only acted as so much oil thrown into the flames. I can not describe to you the effect produced upon the minds of the people throughout the country by the capture of John Caulker and his war party by the Sierra Leone government. The Purrow beast has received a death-wound in its forehead, while slavery in this immediate vicinity is gasping for breath. We missionaries and our little band of converts are filled with joy and gladness, because our ears are constantly being greeted with the sound, "*Allah hoc barro*" (God is great). From the beginning we told the people that this was God's war, and that he would mind all of his people and bring them good out of it. Not one Christian to our knowledge suffered except the women of Koolong. Quite a number of slaves have lost their masters, and three masters who were professors of religion have lost their slaves. The small-pox has been raging in Shengay and the surrounding villages for two months, and is still prevalent. Many have died. As soon as they are taken with it they are carried into the bush, to a farm-house. Many people come from the villages to attend worship, both at Shengay and Bomphetook. The people confess freely that the Purrow is of no use. They say, "God done take the country."

Ten were received into the Church this quarter. We have at Shengay thirty-nine members, all told. Seven are under watch-care. Five of these are women who profess religion but who are the wives of polygamists. Two are men who profess, but we thought best to take them on trial. There are nine in the seekers' class. Two of our members have died this quarter, namely, Peter Stafford and Hannah. When Brother Stafford could no longer speak, he raised his hand and pointed upward, at the same time looking up and smiling.

JOSEPH GOMER.

A WHOLE TOWN PUT TO FLIGHT.

A week ago yesterday Brothers Gomer and Williams and myself started for Turtle Islands to see what opportunity we might find there for doing good. And truly the opportunities are great; for I think I never saw or heard of human beings more degraded than they. At the first two islands at which we stopped there were but few persons living. We talked with them some about God who made them, and Jesus their Savior. From this place we went to the largest town and island of the group. When the people of that place saw me, and saw that we were landing at their town, they all—except one girl who had been to Bomphetook, and had become acquainted with Brother Williams,—became so frightened that they gathered up what things they could carry and ran and hid themselves in the bush, leaving their cassada over the fire cooking. This is the first time I ever knew I was such a terrible-looking object as to put a whole town to flight—especially one having two devil-houses, and medicine hanging at every door and on every tree about the town for the purpose of taking care of them. After considerable search the boatmen found the young chief, or head-man of the town, and got him to come back. We gave him a quenanny, and told him we had not come to harm him or his people, but to do them good, to tell them of God, and that we wanted to stay in his town that night. He gave us permission to stay. We selected a barra as our place for the night, and put up our hammocks to sleep in. We would have had a very comfortable place had it not been for the fleas and the mosquitoes. We set our cook to work to get us something to eat, and sent the chief in search of his people. About eight o'clock he succeeded in getting the greater part of them back, after which we each did some talking. I never witnessed better order or better attention than they gave. The next day we went to another island, about seven miles farther at sea. Here we found a few persons who were in a state of entire nudity. At this place we anchored a little distance at sea, and slept in our boat. The next day about noon we started for home, and got there at dusk Thursday evening. These scenes and this experience makes my soul cry within me, Why is it that there are so few Christian workers here in this dark, benighted land? Oh, why is it? Truly the harvest is great, and the laborers are few. O Lord, send forth more laborers. Trusting in God, I will do the best I can. JOSEPH WOLFE.

March, 1876.

DAVID CASSAMBOE.

On the north bank of the Yaltucher River, about two miles from its mouth, in the midst of the thick bush, is the little village of Mosam. It was in this village that the hero of this story was born; and they called him Kong, because that was his name. It is the custom in that country to call every first boy by that name; and every first girl is called Bwoy.

One day, when little Kong was large enough to run about and get into mischief, his father took him to the Purrow bush and gave him to the Purrow devil. Now the Purrow devil is not that cloven-footed evil spirit that you children dread so much, but a man, one of the chief officers of the society. He took little Kong, anointed him all over with oil, and rubbed him with what they call "lacah," a kind of white clay; and he said his name must be Contam. He is now returned to his mother, with his new name.

Shortly after this Kong's parents heard that some missionaries had come to Shengay, about one day's walk from their place. These missionaries were from America, and had come to teach children to read books, and to *sabba* (know) God. The parents thought they would like for little Kong, or Contam, to learn to read books and to know God; for you must know that they were both heathen at this time, and knew nothing about God. The mother had visited Shengay and attended the meetings held by the missionaries; so she urged that little Kong, or Contam, should be given to the missionaries altogether. The father brought him and gave him to them, and, knowing that missionaries are not Purrow-men, he supposed that a Purrow name would not do; so he asked the king's son what name he must give the boy, and it was agreed that he be called David Cassamboe, as the father's name was Cassamboe.

Little David commenced at once to attend school, and learned very fast to speak English and to read. After he had got so he could read in the Bible he attended the boys' Bible-class, taught by Thomas Caulker, Tuesday nights. On our way home from the class, one night, in answer to my question as to what their lesson was about, he said they "been read 'bout where dem people keep meetin' dey get one gate name Beautiful, an' dem carry one man what no hable for walker and lay him dere to beg dem people for copper [they call all money copper]; and when Peter and John want for go in, he say, 'Come, gie me copper, now.' Peter say, 'I no get, but dat ting what I get I go gie you; get up walk, now.' So he begin for walker." JOSEPH GOMER.

THE BOYS AT SHENGAY.

Among the boys at Shengay, some are very interesting and some have very interesting names. Very often children, when only a few months old, are given to persons living in another village, to be raised, and seldom see their mother or father,—in fact, the father is very little thought of by many. Numbers of the people believe that strangers can raise their children better than the parents. They say that the children will mind strangers better; and this, in many cases, is true, because the parents do not know how to gain their children's love, but say they must whip them to

SHENGAY MISSION CHILDREN BEATING RICE.

make them fear them. Some have one name and some have two.

Garilla is a real smart little fellow, just about a yard high. He can read the Bible, and takes great delight in committing verses to memory and in singing, "We are toiling up the way." Little Garilla is a faithful Sabbath-school pupil, and a great favorite with all who know him.

Harry Yarn is a big boy. His father is the head-man for a country village, and carves wooden gods for the heathen to worship. He carved one which is in the mission-rooms in Dayton, Ohio. Sometimes the school-boys in Shengay laugh at Harry and make fun of him because his father makes wooden gods; but Harry says nothing, for he is a good boy and is trying to be a Christian. He, too, is a dear lover of the Sabbath-school. His father sent him to Shengay to attend the mission-school and to "learn white man's fashion."

Little Tommy Reader was a dear little boy, and his mother is a good woman. She taught Tommy to say his prayers, morning and evening, and to ask a blessing before eating. He used to say he wanted to be a missionary. He would go all through the village and enter the huts and barras, and if he saw people eating he would ask them if they prayed first; if they had not, he would tell them they must pray first and then God would like them, but if they eat without praying God would not like them. Frequently on meeting-nights he would go through the village asking the people to come to the meeting and pray, so the war could not spoil the country. But poor little Tommy was taken sick very suddenly, one day, while playing on the sand-beach, and in a few hours his spirit was with God.

JOSEPH GOMER.

WHAT HAVE WE IN AFRICA?

We have at Shengay a large day-school and a still larger Sunday-school, an organized society of over forty members, and quite a number of others who profess religion,—some of whom are Christians, but are not entirely free from polygamy, slavery, and the Purrow,—who in due time will become members of the Church. There is also here an excellent mission-residence; and there are two chapels,—one in Shengay, which will accommodate one hundred and fifty people, and the neat new stone chapel, on the mission-ground, which accommodates two hundred and twenty. The one hundred and fifty acres of land which we own here constitutes the healthiest and most accessible place on the west coast of Africa, among the heathen proper. At Bomphetook we have an excellent country chapel, and a church of about twenty members. Here too, is both a day and Sunday school. This place is also on the coast, and but fifteen miles farther down than Shengay. A few towns still farther on, and the seven or eight between Bomphetook and Shengay, may all be easily reached; and most of them have been visited occasionally by our missionaries. What have we in Africa? A small but good beginning made, with scores of open doors of usefulness inviting us to enter and convert the people from the error of their ways. We have in Africa thousands of souls to enlighten and save.

Among the number who joined the Church at its first organization in 1874 was a woman named Hannah, a convert who did it amid keen opposition. Her husband beat her severely for joining the Church; but having found Christ precious as a Savior from sin, she continued faithful until death, which occurred nine months afterward. In the beautiful and touching words of Rev. J. W. Hott, how true it was of her that "while her body sunk down into death, her soul rose up higher and higher until it shook hands with Christ and the angels. From the shaded shores of Africa pure spirits are being caught up to God, washed in the blood of the Lamb. Oh, it must be wondrously glorious to get right up out of heathenism, and shake off all its misery and superstition and death, and burst right into the heavenly mansion! I should like to see these poor souls when they first open their eyes on the beauty and bliss of that blessed city of Jesus."

Another one of our members there died, who was saved in the kingdom of grace, and of whom Brother Gomer wrote, "Brother Williams and myself on yesterday attended the funeral of the old mat-maker, Na Yan Kin. She was nearly eighty years of age, and a slave. She died in the faith, trusting in Jesus. When I have more time I wish to write to you of her life, and of her daughter who died a few months ago; how Yan Kin died; how they wrapped her in a mat, tied her to a pole, and buried her two feet deep." This old woman would not attend meeting for a long time, because she had but one eye; but over three years ago she was converted, and abandoned work on the Sabbath-day, and lived a Christian. "From that far-off land souls are going to dwell with Jesus. Some of our missionaries, who were once in Africa, but are now in heaven, must rejoice to see the converted heathen coming to sit down in the kingdom of God." In short, we have a good deal in Africa, and a few souls in heaven, as the results of our labor among the Sherbro people.

TWENTY YEARS AGO.

On the third day of December, 1856, seven missionaries sailed out of New York, bound for the west coast of Africa, and after a long and tedious passage they arrived in this far-off land. One of the number died in less than three months, another returned home in a short time, another continued here some fifteen months and also returned home, another died and was buried in mid-ocean. Two are now in the United States, one is in Scotland, and your humble servant is now in Africa.

Twenty years ago this part of the Sherbro country was without the gospel. Very few had ever heard of a Savior. The grounds upon which the station is built were in bush. The large cotton-tree in front of the mission-house was unapproachable, because "*Medicine live deh.*" I said, "*Nonsense;* cut away the bush; prepare the way for the mission; make the place clean." To-day flowers and fruits are growing on the borders of the walks in the shade of this cotton-tree.

Twenty years ago the town of Shengay was the scene of cruelties such as are common to a heathen people. The Purrow was in full force. The Purrow devil lived like a prince until your humble servant frightened him out of his wits one night, when he ran into the bush. To-day the Purrow does not control the common people.

Twenty years ago the Christian Sabbath was not known. No religious services had been held; Christ had not been preached to the people. To-day the Sabbath is better observed there than in France, or even in portions of New York City. To-day men, women, and children assemble for morning prayers and services at 10:00 A. M., Sunday-school at 3:00 P. M., and services again in the evening. The "tom-tom," or African drum, is not heard on the Sabbath as it was twenty years ago.

Eighteen years ago, while building the mission-house, I had a law forbidding any one in the employment of the mission to go to Shengay on the Sabbath to "beat drum" or dance. That law was violated by one Bgannah. On Monday morning "Tong" came and told me what had been done. I called all the people and explained again why the law had been made, and wherein it had now been violated. I felt it to be a very serious case, and by the aid of the Holy Spirit was enabled to so impress the wrongfulness of this violation of mission-law on the minds of the young men that they not only asked my forgiveness, but also begged God's mercy. Eleven young men gave their names, expressing a willingness to receive the truth. Among the number was "Tong," a heathen boy, now Thomas Tucker, a Christian man. Oh, what a transformation! From Tong to Thomas is nothing, but from heathen Tong to Christian Thomas is something. This Thomas is not only a Christian in name, but in fact. This is the most wonderful and best part of it. Twenty years ago the dark night of ignorance covered the minds of the people. To-day pen, ink, and paper, newspapers and books, are in requisition. J. K. BILLHEIMER.

Shengay Station, West Africa, January 3, 1877.

MISSION STOCK, VISIT TO MAMBO AND MASSAMA.

The canoe, with the mission stock of six head of cattle, five sheep, and one horse, landed at the mission on the 10th. The sea was rough, and one of the cattle got sick crossing the bay and died in the night. The rest are now doing well. We put the yoke on the oxen yesterday for the first time. They are like many of the people—do everything wrong, and do not want to work. This part of the work I have to trust wholly to Mr. Keen, an American colored man that I have hired. When I came from Freetown last week I brought with me Mr. Hero, a man fifty-two years of age, and an ordained minister. He has been preaching nineteen years; was eleven years a missionary on McCarthy's Island, and taught school thirteen years in Sierra Leone in his early life. He has been with us two Sabbaths. He preaches well. He is a native African. He—with his wife's assistance, who is a good Christian woman, —is to teach school and preach at Mambo, the mission of the Dayton, Ohio, Summit Street Sabbath-school. He came with me just to see how he liked the place, and how we should like him.

Yesterday I went up with him to Mambo. Our chief, George Caulker, gave me a letter to Prince William, but he was not at home. The Purrow devil had caught his young brother—the one that came to see us about the school—and had him in the Purrow bush. The house the chief is building is not finished, but Bannah Boom, the head-man of the town, promised to give Mr. Hero a house until the chief returns.

When we went to Massama, in the Great Scarces River, in the Timiny country, in search of cattle for the mission, King Bey Farmer received us very cordially. A curious kind of brass image, and one of clay, stood at the entrance of his hut. These were made by the French, and sold to the king. The people here are a mixture of Mohammedans and Kaffres. The king is a Mohammedan. I gave him an Arabic Bible. His brother is a priest. I preached in the mosque at night. The place could not contain all the people. After speaking a short time on the creation of man, his fall, and Christ the Savior, they all shouted, "Talk more. We can't deny the word. Talk again. We are glad for this word. Tell me plenty!" The king himself arose and made quite a speech. Early the next morning—Sabbath morning—the king came to my house and asked me to go with him to the grave of his son and kill a cow,—all cattle are cows with the Africans,—and help to make sacrifice at the grave. As I was a big foda I must offer the sacrifice. His son had been dead twenty days. He was a stranger in the place where he had gone. The people there would ask him where he came from, and what he bring to eat, and a lot of such talk. I saw plainly this was a trick of the devil to spoil my meeting here to-day. The Mohammedan priests present at the meeting saw the situation, and this sacrifice was a trick of theirs. At 11:00 A. M. I had a meeting, and but few were present. Most of them went with the king. In the afternoon I went by land to Gambia, distant about five miles. The old king, San Alimammi Labare, received me very kindly. This is a very large town; not less than 2,000 people. They got up a large meeting in the king's yard. He begged me hard to hold meetings there all the time. J. GOMER.

RECEPTION OF MISSIONARIES.

As all the other missionaries have written of our journey, I come in last. We are now at the end of our voyage. We left Freetown on Friday, December 22d, and when nearing the mission cannon were fired in Shengay. The king has two brass cannon, and four salutes were fired from them. Brother Wolfe having preceded us had the large American flag run up, and also a small one, displaying their beautiful stars and stripes from the top of the oleander-tree. A large crowd of men, women, and children met us at the wharf, and we were borne ashore amid deafening shouts, hurrahs, and cheering. It made us think of the reception we received on our return to America, minus the refreshments and speeches.

Sabbath morning Flickinger Chapel was well filled. People were there from Shooney, Cattah, and Tissanah. We were welcomed on entering with a song by the school-children. The Sabbath-school and evening services were also well attended. Our service on Christmas was very interesting. We had a Christmas-tree at night, with a present for most of the people, and speaking by the children. Mr. Gomer and myself attended two meetings last Sabbath morning, one at Shooney and one at Cattah. Brother Wolfe preached at Shengay at 11:00 A. M. Mr. Billheimer arrived at our mission-wharf yesterday about 9:00 A. M., remained during the day, and conducted the prayer-meeting in Shengay at night. We are having a week of prayer. We have just returned from prayer-meeting. The subject for to-night was woman's missionary work, and missionary work generally. We are all enjoying good health, except Brother Wolfe. He is suffering very much. Remember us ever in your prayers.

MARY W. GOMER.

ABOUT THINGS IN AFRICA.

You would laugh to see what queer little houses the people live in. They are built of sticks and daubed with mud. I have seen some not larger than ten feet square. People seem to live in them peaceably and happily; indeed, they *must* be peaceable or such a wee bit of a house would not hold them. You will be surprised when I tell you that the women do most of the building. The men put up the frame-work of sticks and the women do the daubing or plastering.

The other evening I went out for a walk; and what do you think I saw? A great stream of ants that the people call "drivers." The reason they gave them such a strange name is, they driv out everything where they are, such as rats, mice, lizzards, centipedes, etc. Even elephants and boa-constrictors fear them. It is said that they will kill and eat up the largest animals. One alone can not do so much; neither can two, nor half a dozen; but they club together, and in that way accomplish what a few could not do. It would be well for us, in doing good, to follow their example.

How would you like to be drawn in a baby-carriage wherever you go? Well, that is about the way *we* travel in Africa. We do not have baby-carriages, but something almost like them; we have "sedan-chairs," and they are drawn by the natives. The sun shines so hot here that we can not walk as much as we can in a colder country.

Only about two hundred feet from the mission-house, near the sea, stands a grand old cotton-tree. Just now it is covered with beautiful white cotton. The people here do not like the cotton that grows on trees. They think if they use it in pillows, and sleep on them, it will make them crazy.

Not long ago I visited the school at Shengay, and saw a monkey in an oleander-tree. As soon as he saw me he scampered down and came right to me. When he saw that I had nothing for him he ran away, climbed up on the back of a bench where one of the children was standing, and commenced picking in her hair as if looking for something.

We have eleven goats here. Sometimes they supply us with milk. Just now they give none.

A. LIZZIE BOWMAN.

SHENGAY NIGHT-SCHOOL, BOMPHETOOK, ROTUFUNK.

This school was organized early in February, in the dining-room of the mission-house, with twenty-one scholars. The second night the room was crowded—chairs and benches all full; and many sat on the floor, so that it was difficult to get about to teach them. So many continued to attend that it was necessary to remove the school to the chapel. There are now sixty scholars enrolled. Willie Caulker, the chief's son, is assistant teacher. His wife is in one of my classes, and is an interesting woman. Several women attend the school. Some bring their babies with them. These are placed on the floor and left to amuse themselves while their mothers study. The little ones are usually very good, and seem as happy in school as their parents. Could the friends of the Woman's Missionary Association witness these Sherbro women poring over their books, they would no doubt feel greatly encouraged to press on in their efforts to enlighten and save them.

The school was opened for the purpose of teaching the people to read the Bible for themselves. Many who are obliged to work during the day, and others too old to attend the day-school, are glad to avail themselves of this opportunity. Gospel seed is sown every school-night. I read a portion of scripture, which is interpreted into Sherbro, as is also the prayer. Sometimes Mr. Thomas Tucker, who is a member of the school, leads in prayer in the Sherbro language.

I came to Bomphetook on the 1st of May, and found an interesting day-school and Sunday-school. There are between twenty and thirty pupils in the day-school, and, I think, over thirty in the Sabbath-school. I have charge of the night-school four nights a week. It is in a flourishing condition. I have a sewing-class of eight. They meet to sew for about an hour four days a week. On Wednesday evening we have prayer-meeting, which is usually well attended, twenty-eight being there last night. So also is the meeting Sunday evenings. There is a boy by the name of John Williams, thirteen years of age, who has helped me much in the night-school, bringing in scholars. Sometimes he takes part in the prayer-meetings. We have another John, whose father is a rum-seller. He is one of the best scholars in school. He has also prayed in meeting

If we succeed in getting established at Rotufunk, the ladies will have the finest station of the Sherbro Mission. The prospect is bright for accomplishing a great work at that place.

E. BEEKEN.

May 31, 1877.

PULLING THE BUNDOO.

A country-woman who is the mistress of a white trader at Boonth came here and asked the chief, George Caulker, that the Bundoo women might pull her, as they call it, out of the Bundoo. Some years ago she was put in the Bundoo-bush and was rubbed with the clay, but was never properly pulled, which is quite a long ceremony of singing, dancing, and drinking rum. The head Bundoo-woman must carry a hamper of the medicines on her head, in the procession. The head-woman for these parts lives at Shengay and is a faithful member of our church. You received her when you dedicated the chapel here. The chief said he would not allow anything of the kind in Shengay. She then went to Debia and got permission from the head-woman to be pulled there. Debia, you know, is but a short mile from Shenguy. She then came here for Keffay Mehany, the old head-woman, to carry the "blie," or hamper. Keffay refused to go, saying she had no business there again, as she had "done leff dat long time."

She got others to try to persuade her, but in vain. The woman then returned to Debia, got a party of women, and came and took her by force. This was on Thursday afternoon, the 18th. At the prayer-meeting that night the women discussed the matter, and after the meeting was over they went to Debia and brought her back by force. Keffay was frightened, and was very much afraid I would turn her out of the meeting. She got some of the members to go into the chapel and pray for her. This woman was what they call only a half Bundoo, and if she should die without being pulled could only go half way to where she wants to go. In the next world she could see her people, but could not go to or talk with them.

Yours truly.   Joseph Gomer.

SUNDAY-SCHOOL WORKERS IN AFRICA.

Bro. F.:—As one of the first-fruits of our children's weekly prayer-meetings, our Sunday-school is perhaps one of the most interesting gatherings we have on the Sabbath. The children under our instruction for the past two years are rendering us very valuable help. They are to be seen every Sunday morning or afternoon in the huts, telling of Jesus to the children, inviting them to school, reproving Sabbath-breaking, and pleading with parents to send their children with them to Sunday-school. They are even inviting adults, and have been successful in bringing in both young and old. A few weeks ago some of them got into Kabby's hut, and invited him and Kong, his companion, to come to Sunday-school. After finding they would take no denial, to get rid of them both men promised to come out. The children offered to wait for them. After waiting, and further talk with them, Kabby and his companion accompanied them. While preparing to leave the house for the school, I heard a noise at the barra gate. In looking out I saw several boys very good-humoredly holding to Kong and pulling him. On inquiring as to the cause, I was informed that Kong had promised to come to Sunday-school, and came thus far to "fool" them, and they do not " gree for that;" so I settled the pleasing palaver by deciding that since Kong had promised them, and came this far, the boys had got the best, and he should go in. Both Kabby and Kong then went in. They came back the following Sabbath, and since then Kabby has attended regularly, while Kong was from home. Last Sabbath Kabby said to Mr. Campbell, the teacher: "I like to come here; put down my name; I shall attend every Sunday." He comes to see me every day. He is here now, helping to re-roof the barra. I have hope in him. Yours in Christ.

J. M. WILLIAMS.

BOMPHETOOK, MAMBO, AND SHENGAY.

We all reached the mission, December 28d, in good health. The following week we held a meeting to lay plans. On the 6th, Mrs. Gomer and myself went to Bomphetook. The school examination was good. The children have made fine progress in grammar, arithmetic, and writing. Mr. Lefever, who was one of the examiners, was so well pleased that he laid eight silver half crowns —one pound—on the table for the benefit of the school. Brother Williams and Mr. Campbell, the teacher, deserve credit. They have a very good school. On the 9th, my wife and I went to Good Hope, where we saw Mr. Root and Mr. Menzies, and talked about the industrial school. I am just from Mambo, where the chief showed me one of their places of worship. The skulls of the African buffalo, baboon, deer, bush-cow, and bush-hogs, and other bones, were all in a heap. Persons with "bad sickness" come to this place, offer a sacrifice, and then they will get well. Hunters also worship here that they may have *success.*

Children are born with the following names: The first son is called Cho; the second, Tong; the third, Saw; the fourth, Barkey; the fifth, Ricah; the sixth, Kotong. The first girl is named

Bay; the second, Yameki, or Yarkie; the third, Conah; the fourth, My-hen; the fifth, Nebang, the sixth, Manneh. The Purrow, Bundoo, or Yassa always change these names, and we often change their names. A head-man sent me a large bundle of witch-medicine recently. The bell for Bomphetook is up, and does well. There are twenty-three laborers and seven children who attend morning worship and take part. Miss Bowman is teaching a sewing-class and managing the mission-children, and Miss Beeken is at Bomphetook. The schools at both Shengay and Bomphetook, and the work generally, are doing well. We greatly need help. Another minister should be sent out immediately. J. GOMER.

SHENGAY MISSION-HOUSE, WEST AFRICA.

We have seventeen and one half acres of ground cleared, and nearly all is planted in cassada, corn, cocoa, yams, arrow-root, and cotton. The stock is all looking well. Both yoke of oxen do well, hauling logs in clearing the farm. We have one milch cow, seventeen sheep and goats, and two hogs. The fishing-seine is a good investment. Tom went out one afternoon, and came back next morning with three hundred and seventy-four pounds of nice fish.

May 13th we received six into the Church

—four males and two females. There are now thirteen on the seekers' list. The Sabbath-school average for the quarter was seventy-nine; day-school, thirty eight. We have now in the mission at Shengay ten boys and two girls. They work from 6:15 to 9:00 A. M., and from 3:30 to 5:30 P. M. I had to stop work on the boys' home to clear ground and plant, but will resume again next week. At present they occupy rooms in the laborers' houses, which are finished.

May 28th, Rev. Mr. Hero went up to Mambo to labor as a school-teacher and a preacher. I was up there on the 16th instant and visited three of the villages near there. On account of the Purrow being in session, not much could be done in the way of teaching and preaching. A little boy, a son of the chief, told me that the devil came into the meeting one Sabbath.

We have made out a plan for itinerating in the villages near Shengay—the farthest not more than twelve miles away. The plan includes ten villages outside of Shengay. Five of our young men, members of the Church, have volunteered to go out, each taking their regular turns. When I have more time I will send you the plan.

At Mambo the woman's work is prospering, though the school is small and the teacher has no proper house to live in. The people are real hungry for the gospel. Nine have joined the seekers' class, and the meetings are very encouraging. Mr. Allen was there last Sabbath, and reports a very interesting meeting. I think we have nothing to fear but much to hope for in the future. Though discouragements arise, they shall vanish away. JOSEPH GOMER.

May, 31, 1877.

MAMBO, WEST AFRICA.

This is a native town about ten miles from Shengay. The chief, Mr. Caulker, and Mr. Hero, our missionary at this place, came to meet us at the wharf. Mrs. Hero was with me.

We do most of our traveling in boats; and it is quite a pleasant way, especially when the wind and tide are in our favor.

It is customary to give a present to the chief or head-man on entering a place—"to shake his hand." Meantime the "strangers" go to the "barra," and wait till he comes. He sends his people to empty a house, which is given to them to use as long as they stay in the place. On leaving the town a "good-by" present is given to the "stranger;" which consists usually of rice, fowls, and occasionally a sheep, goat, or bullock, where they have these. I did not think it necessary to give a present on coming here; but the head-man told the chief that the white woman had come, but she had not given them anything to shake their hand. I got the present at the "eleventh hour," and gave it to him.

The "Purrow" is in full operation at present. On Tuesday the boys were brought out of the "bush" where they had been kept for nine months. There were one hundred and fifteen in all who were initiated. These boys are not allowed to see their friends during the time they are in the "bush;" and it is a fearful thing for any one who is not a Purrow-man to enter it at all.

Two of our boys want me to say "good-how-do" for them, to the boys and girls away over the sea. One asked me why no white children ever come here from America.

A. Lizzie Bowman

June 1, 1877.

CHAPTER XLVIII.

WHAT WE CAN AND OUGHT TO HAVE, SOON, IN AFRICA.

In this chapter we propose to sketch in a brief manner the work we ought next to accomplish in Africa. The implements, and all that was thought to be necessary for the purpose of putting the industrial school into successful operation, were sent to Africa early this year. The preparatory work—such as clearing the ground, building houses for shops and lodging-rooms, obtaining seeds and plants, and making arrangements to furnish suitable labor for girls, as well as for boys, —has already been largely done. This has given our missionaries much additional care; and but for the fact that there exists a real necessity for such an enterprise, it ought never have been undertaken. But it is absolutely necessary to furnish employment for our advanced pupils in the schools, and for converts who wish to make a respectable living in some legitimate business. If they must pursue some heathen occupation, and do this as they do it, and among them, a large per cent of them will go back to heathenism. Besides, to show the people that there is a better way will be a great inducement to them to forsake their heathenism. The introduction of agricultural and mechanical pursuits, such as will develop the resources of the country and the skill and industry of the people, and increase their wealth, will tend much to give them nobler views of life, and in every way qualify them to both produce and consume profitably more than they now do, or even know of. They have numerous real wants, physical, intellectual, moral, and religious, which they will be made to realize only as civilization and Christianity cause them to see them. These will develop the resources of soil and brain found in that country, and contribute largely to the growth of commerce, science, and literature. The world is beginning to recognize this fact, and appreciates the worth of Christian missions, because they have contributed so largely to these. It would know but little of the geography, languages, and real condition of the people of most heathen lands but for the knowledge which it has obtained through missionaries.

The primary object of Christian missions to the heathen is to teach them their duty to God, and as far as possible induce them to discharge it; but other important ends should be and mostly are accomplished, such as have been alluded to in this chapter. It should be our aim to make thorough work in Africa, and not allow it to be but partially or imperfectly done. To do this will require time, effort, money—especially the latter; and if this be forthcoming as the demands of the work require, the amount of effort and time necessary to bring about the end desired will be much less than if the work has to be carried forward under constant financial embarrassment, as has been the case often in the past.

With the rich country we have there,—rich in material resources, and richer still in its mental and moral possibilities,—we ought more rapidly to subdue that land to Christ. To plead inability is to excuse ourselves upon false grounds. Did all act their part as well as some do in contributing funds, at least threefold more would be secured. To withhold or to give parsimoniously while millions are wholly destitute of the gospel of Christ, and the command to preach it to every creature stands unrepealed, is certainly a sin against God.

The discouragements growing out of our not having money to man the African mission properly have been the greatest we have had to contend with in its entire history. True, there have been serious obstacles in the way, and at times it looked as though they were such as would crush it. More than once, when without any protection, war parties came near it, who could have destroyed its buildings, as no one was there to resist them. Truly a wonderful providence has watched over that mission from its origin. The change that came over Chief Caulker, who was induced to give us so favorable a location, after refusing it for nearly two years, and which caused him at his advanced age, and after having been so much opposed to the mission and Christianity, to become a Christian himself, and its warmest friend, is indeed remarkable.

The leadings of Providence certainly indicate that there should be great energy shown in the prosecution of the work in Africa.

APPENDIX.

CHAPTER XLIX.

[The author has visited Africa twice since 1877, and most of what follows was written by the missionaries and himself while there. The account given of the progress of the work, including the woman's mission, with the author's report to the Board in May, 1882, show what has been and what still needs to be done in that dark land.]

WHAT THE CHIEF SAID.

Sourie Cassabe the chief at Rotufunk told me several times that if I would come and sit down close to him he would "hold all the word what I tell him, because he see it good." When Brother Wolfe and myself were first there he asked how he must do to be saved. He says if I were there I could show him "all how to mind them people." And many others say they would be glad to have the word, if they could get any person to show them. It does *me* good to show them. Mr. Green is hauling stone with the oxen on a sled which Mr. Wolfe had made. The stones are to protect the bank where the wall is broken again. Yesterday some natives from one of the rivers, after watching the cattle for some time, said, "Dem cow him work. Oh, I hear say dem kin dig ground. I want to see um." I told them it was not the time now to dig ground. The leopards got among our goats and killed several; also one pig. A calf was attacked just in front of the mission-house one night. It made so much noise that it awoke us all. So with a lantern in one hand and a revolver in the other I started to the rescue; but fearing the leopard might prove more than a match for me, I fired at it before I reached it. This frightened it off; but the calf was so badly bitten that we had to kill it. The cow got sick, and we had to kill her. The goats, pig, and calf were all killed inside of two weeks, and the sow and two pigs died.

JOSEPH GOMER.

August 6, 1877.

AFRICAN INCIDENT.

The lesson was Acts xiv. 8–20. "I asked my class why Paul and Barnabas did not accept of the honors the people wished to bestow upon them; could they think of any one mentioned in the Bible who accepted of praise or honor? One remembered a king who wore his fine clothes and made a speech to the people, and they said he was a god. Humphi said he remembered one fine gentleman who got one bad sick that he not hable to cure, and been one little gal there with his wife, what come out far country. She tell his wife dey one man in her country what hable for doctor um. So he take plenty of money and he come to the man. The man tell um, say, Go wash yourself; and he vex for that. And his servant tell him, say, What matter you no want to wash? So he wash, and he get better just now."

The head-man of Tissanna sent, last week, to tell me that if they die and God asks them why they do not keep meeting there on Sundays they will tell him that we Shengay people were to blame for that. At Sandoo, Senehoo, Bonthe, and Mambo they sent, saying that we must come to them all the time.   JOSEPH GOMER.
September, 1877.

TWENTY-FIVE YEARS IN AFRICA.

I have been much interested in the new industrial work that is being begun by Mr. Gomer at Shengay. That has been my idea of missionary work in Africa for a quarter of a century. Though laboring under great discouragements, I have been permitted to experience gratifying results. Of the twenty-four children—twelve boys and twelve girls—taken into the industrial school at Good Hope twenty-two years ago, four have died, leaving the best of evidence that they were converted and have gone to heaven. One of them graduated with honors at an American college and returned to his people as a Christian minister, and till the day of his death maintained the character of an educated Christian gentleman. One young man from that family was employed by Mr. Gomer as teacher at Shengay, and for a number of years was often spoken of by Mr. Gomer as a valuable assistant. Another young man from that family has been for many years, and is still, a faithful and efficient teacher in the Mendi mission-schools. All the boys of the family were taught the use of tools, and several of them became very skillful mechanics. With their help alone, and the heathen laborers, I was enabled to build a saw-mill,—a picture of which you once gave in the *Missionary Visitor*. From that time to the present the mill has held a prominent place in the industrial department of the mission. Five of the girls of that family were respectably married, and settled near the mission. Three girls were sent home to their friends because of immoral conduct. One boy was sent to his father for inefficiency. All the girls of the family were taught all branches connected with housekeeping, and in needle-work they excelled, both in plain and fancy sewing; and from the time that they became large enough to do the work, no other help was employed in the house. I would say to your people, Keep on, and sustain Mr. Gomer in his industrial work. God will bless it, and eternity will show that it is labor well spent. Yours for the blessed cause.

D. W. BURTON.

Plymouth, Illinois, September 3, 1877.

BISHOP HAVEN AND LIBERIA.

Bishop Haven, of the Methodist Episcopal Church, who visited Liberia November 1877, says of that people, who are only two hundred miles south of Shengay:

"There are about twenty thousand colored Americans. The native population is about four hundred thousand. The American population is found chiefly in about six towns on the coast. The natives are heathens, of course. They have no forms of civilization. They go in a nude state. There is no relation between the natives and the colored Americans. They are just as industrious as any class of people who live in the tropical countries. The frosts of the North give northerners a start ahead of southerners. The Liberians I met are quite industrious, and in business transactions are quite shrewd. Some of the largest merchants are colored men. They own farms up the St. Johns and St. Paul's rivers. Hundreds of acres of land have been cleared and cultivated. Liberia, like all other countries that are poor, needs money. There is a clause in the constitution prohibiting white men from owning any land. They were afraid that the white man would run them out. They want his money, but do not want him. I think that he will eventually be allowed to buy land there. They want and must have industries and railroads there; therefore some person must furnish the capital. Africa is a beautiful and wealthy country. I think the African mind is susceptible of the highest forms of education. Of course, all people in warm countries suffer from the heat, but they are not necessarily incapable of an advanced degree of culture. Africa will be civilized by religion, commerce, and politics. The means of communication with the outside world are increasing all the time. It only takes fifteen days from Monrovia to England."

AN IMAGE—MOHAMMEDAN.

We are all in very good health this morning. Miss Beeken, Mr. Campbell, and myself left here on the 2d for Rotufunk. I spent the night with Richard Caulker, at Tangahnahma (that is, sweet cassava). Miss Beeken went on and slept at Canolo (that means, under a sassy-tree). Next day at 8:00 P. M. we were at Rotufunk. At night we had a very interesting meeting. The Mohammedans were having a big meeting also. It is a fast-month with them. They must fast until they see the new moon, which will be about the 8th or 9th. The king of the Quiah country, Fouray-Dugoo, and Mahara, was here. He is a great man in the country. He was sent here by the governor of Sierra Leone to settle some war-palaver. He is a Mohammedan and a good Arabic scholar. His son, a fine young man, is not a Mohammedan, and received an English education in Freetown. He invited the people to the meeting, and interpreted for us. Mr. Campbell spoke well from I. Tim. ii. 5. I followed, speaking on the birth of Christ. Next morning King Allemammy sent to know if we would hold a meeting at his place. So when he had sent the Mohammedans away, except a few, and four of his wives, together with a few of the towns-people, we all went over and explained to them the sufferings and death of Christ—after which they sent us letters, which I forward to you. Eight of the king's wives were there in the town, but only four attended the meeting.

Early the next morning after we reached Rotu-funk, I was standing in front of the house. A girl passed, going toward the river, with an image ornamented with beads in her hand. I asked her to show it to me, and offered to buy it. She said it was a woman's child, and she was going to wash it. She refused to sell it. I spoke to the king, asking him to get it for me. He sent for the woman, who said that she gave birth to twins, and one died. She had this image made, and believed that the spirit of the dead child now dwelt in it and minded the family. She could not part with it. I had taken my revolver with me —the one presented to me in New York. I showed it to the king, and told him if he would get the image for me I would give him the revolver, and an Arabic Bible for his friend, who wanted one. He saw the husband, and they began making country fashion and offering sacrifices, I suppose to get the spirit out of the image. By two o'clock next day Foora Boandoo, the king's son, brought it to me. He had worked hard to get it for me, and I promised to send him an English Bible. This was his greatest wish. I send the image to you just as I saw it in the girl's hands. JOSEPH GOMER.

October 2, 1877.

ROTUFUNK, WEST AFRICA.

I came here yesterday and found the buildings about the same as Mr. Gomer represented them as being when he left here seven weeks ago. Mr. Gomer left one of his carpenters here then, to make the window-cases and shutters. The latter only are made. You see how slowly work will go when left to native discretion.

AFRICAN IMAGE.

The chief went to work last Saturday morning with a strong force, putting the roof on and daubing the house. He works the same as any of his people—in the mud to his knees. I was at the house this forenoon, and saw him at work. So I gave him "Tankie, tankie." He said he would not daub a house for himself, but this house was for God and he would work for him. I was up to the house just before night, and found the roof all on and the first coat of mud. I fear the carpenter-work will keep us back most. I shall try and get them at work building the barra in a day or two. I do not intend leaving here until the buildings are ready to use, if my health does not fail. I use my hammock for my bed, as otherwise I would have to use the ground-floor.

I had a very large and attentive congregation here. Two chiefs attended it, and quite a number of Mohammedans, who gave their sanction to much that I said. A son of one of the chiefs, who was educated in Freetown, interpreted for me.

In the afternoon I went to quite a large town some distance up the river. Here I met a number of people; but the chief would not allow me to speak until he had given me a present of some rice and a fowl. Then he said I could speak. I told him my errand, and he called the people together. There were upward of a hundred, who listened very attentively. When I left, the chief urged me to come again.

JOSEPH WOLFE.

November 25, 1877.

EXTRACTS FROM A LETTER TO A SABBATH-SCHOOL.

I have not time to tell you all I know; but the Purrow-devil—I must tell you all about that. They have a devil-bush at a town a few miles from here. They dress up men to represent devils, and send them out to catch men and boys. They will not have women. The children at Shengay all look anxiously forward to Christmas as a great gala-day; and all like to dress up on that day. For several weeks the boys have been begging for work to do, that they may buy clothes to wear. Some want shirts, some jumpers, some hats. Four or five shillings will buy a suit such as they want. I gave a job to two of our Sabbath-school boys, that they might get jumpers to wear Christmas. Just as they had finished the work one of the devils came and caught them and several other of our Sabbath-school children, and carried them to this bush, where they must stay perhaps for several months. The king was at Bendoo. I went to see him and protested against such unlawful proceedings. He said he had no power over the Purrow. I told him that then we must appeal to a King who did have power over it. This we are doing every day. We are praying to the King of heaven and earth, to put a stop to these heathen practices. Will you not unite your prayers with ours that God may put an end to the Purrow-devil. This is the first we have had so close here for five years, and the people do not wish it. It is only a few wicked men, who hate the mission and everything that is good, that have brought it here.

JOSEPH GOMER.

December 17, 1877.

HELP NEEDED.

It is time for my quarterly report; but I beg you will excuse me this quarter, and I hope Mr. Wilberforce will be here by the time the next is due. I am just as busy as I can be from early in the morning until late at night. We are clearing and plowing for our fall crops. We are now plowing with two yoke of oxen. I am head plowman. It takes three of us,—one to hold the plow and two to drive,—as the cattle are not well broken. In the schools and religious department all is going as well as could be expected. At Shengay our day-meetings are thinly attended. The day-school has an attendance of from thirty-five to fifty. Birds must be driven from rice. We might have a good night-school but for the expense. Of the nine that we received into the church lately, six were mission-boys between twelve and sixteen years of age. There is, I am happy to say, quite a religious interest among the boys in the mission. Every Saturday night the boys have their own prayer-meeting in their house. I have never attended their meeting. It is purely their own. It has been going on for several months. At Bomphetook the work is at a stand-still. At Manoh it is very encouraging. Two weeks ago I spent a Sabbath there and at Thumbah. Mrs. Curtis has a large and interesting class of seekers, who meet every Sabbath morning and once a week for prayers. Our meetings there were well attended; twenty-seven attended the Sabbath-school; the daily attendance at day-school is from twelve to sixteen. She has a night-school for adults that is well attended, only they do not come regularly. The people are very kind to Mrs. Curtis, and help her much with food. At Mambo we have much to be thankful for. Both church and school are doing well. My health is very good. Mr. Sawyer is performing well his part of teacher and preacher. My greatest need now is for some one who can manage a farm and who understands cattle. I am so tired when night comes; but relief will come. The school-children have several bushels of kernels to pay for their *Visitors* again.

The spiritual work of the mission has never yet had a better prospect than it now has. Early at the commencement of the dry season there were several Purrow-bushes established throughout the different villages by a few wicked men who hate the gospel, for the one purpose of retarding its progress; and they succeeded, in a measure, in lessening the attendance at the meetings. Many of the school-children were caught and forced into the Purrow-bush; and in some cases some of the members had been taken by force and put there, even from their houses. Such extreme measures have done harm to their own cause. We frequently hear some of their own people say, "This thing pass mark;" and many of them speak openly against it, saying, "I never wish to see Purrow here again." A few years ago it was their glory to belong to the Purrow; but of late years, and even now, many are ashamed to be associated with it.

All through the country the people are willing to come and keep meeting on Sunday. Truly, the people are hungry for the gospel; but we have not force enough to send it to them. We are doing all that we can to give it to as many as possible.

I feel that we must open two more schools in connection with our work here,—one at Manoh and one at Thumbah. At both of these places they have given us good houses. For the present they will not cost over one hundred dollars a year for each school. I know that you are hard pushed for means; but if I can have my health to go about after Mr. Wilberforce comes I can raise the money here. If none of the Sabbath-schools in America will support these schools, we will volunteer to do so. By the time the Board meets these schools will be in operation, God willing.

I am just on the eve of starting to Freetown now for the doctor, but hope to be back in a week or ten days. My sickness began with erysipelas and terminated in yellow jaundice. For ten days I have been helpless. My wife has done her best in the way of doctoring, but to no purpose. All medicines seem to have lost their power.

I forgot to state in the proper place that we have dropped six members from our church-rolls for participating in the Purrow, and six were dismissed for other causes. We now have fifty-eight members at Shengay. There are eight members in the church at Bomphetook. The field looks very inviting, if we can only get the help. I trust we shall yet gather many precious sheaves.

I am longing for Mr. Wilberforce to come and help me. JOSEPH GOMER.
April, 1878.

FIFTY YEARS AGO.

After crossing Yahrah Bay, the first point and the most westerly of the mainland of the Sherbro country is Shengay, where the Sherbro Mission is located. About two miles west of the mainland are the famous Plantain Islands,—famous for having once been the fortified residence of the late King Caulker. Fifty years ago the foreign as well as the domestic slave-trade was in full operation on this part of the coast. King Caulker was largely engaged in this business. Out of the money he obtained from the sale of his people he built a handsome and substantial stone structure on the largest of these islands, as well as a fort of no mean pretensions, upon which were mounted cannon. Here the unfortunate wretches who were taken in war and in other ways were confined until a sufficient number had been collected to constitute a cargo for the slave-trader. But King Caulker is dead and gone, and his works do follow him. The island was long since deserted. Time, wind, and tide have demolished houses and fort. The writer himself had some of the stones removed from the king's palace and had them placed in the walls of the mission-house at Shengay. The steps on which the people ascend to the residence of our missionaries at Shengay were built from stones removed from these ruins. J. K. BILLHEIMER.

INDUSTRIAL FARM — MRS. GOMER'S CLASS.

This industrial farm is a pretty big undertaking, —larger than I had expected,—and it requires very close watching of both the men and the boys; but I believe we shall make it pay this year. I find we must have fences—and only live fences will do here. I am planting Bahama-grass to pasture the cattle, as none of the other seed grew. Our blacksmith has made a cart that we work the oxen to. We use it to do our hauling, and it saves much labor. The smith proves to be a very profitable man. Besides doing all our work he does a great deal for outside parties, from which we get a profit. People come from far away to get work done. Our mission is becoming very popular in the country. I do very much wish that you could come out with Mr. Wilberforce. I would be willing to contribute a good part of the expenses out of my own salary. If you can not come yourself, let some other person come who understands farming, and who would visit all the stations. And it would be nice if while here you would organize the Church at Mambo. There will be material there. On my return from Rotufunk, I stopped at Bomphetown. The chief is still calling for a school at his town. I think there should be one somewhere in that vicinity. The rain came very early this year, before the people got their farms burned.

The box of clothing and books sent from Lewisburg was received in good order. We were truly thankful, especially for the clothes, as they were all made up ready for the children. Mrs. Gomer has had her hands full since Miss Bowman left. She, with what little help one of the girls could give, has done all of the sewing for all these children. Besides, she has organized a class of seven little girls, which is called the Lewisburg Class. All are dressed from the box above referred to. Every Sabbath she teaches them in the Sabbath-school. Here are their names: Hannah Curtis, Dorcas John, Moro, Choco Myany, Mima, Bay, and Mayhen. You will see that all have not got English names yet. Every Sabbath plenty of children flock to her class, but she sends them all away but her seven. Dorcas John and Hannah Curtis live in the mission. Every morning and evening Dorcas prays for her mother and her mother's brother, for Brother John Try, who lives at Manoh, for the people who are taking care of her, for her teacher, and for all the good people in America who send them books and clothing. She is about six years old. Words can not express our thanks for the clothing sent.

JOSEPH GOMER.

Shengay, West Africa, June 7, 1878.

WHAT OUR AGENT SAID.

Rev. W. Wicklethwaite, who with his wife visited Shengay some time last month on the occasion of the anniversary, had given such glowing accounts of the progress of the work there that others besides myself to whom he described things he saw there could not but be highly and agreeably interested. I hope it will so continue, and be furthered on, and that Mr. Wilberforce, who is reported as coming out, will soon be here, to enable Mr. Gomer to extend his work, as he seems determined to do; for in its worldly as well as its spiritual aspect the mission is silently taking hold upon the people and changing their habits for good. It can not stop there; and your mission appears to me to be destined to accomplish still greater results in this part of Africa.

I. FITZJOHN.

Sierra Leone, West Africa, July 10, 1878.

SHENGAY SNAKE, RAT, AND CAT STORY.
[Written to Sunday-school children.]

Children usually like stories; so I will give you a snake and cat story, with a few rats mixed in. The rats were very bad in our rice-store, so I sent for a dozen cats to catch them. Tom brought home three the first day and put them in the store. One refused to stay there, and came over to the mission-house. The next morning one of the laborers, while sweeping the store, looked under the rice-bin, and gave a fearful yell and ran out of the store, saying there was one "boom, boom uker" (big, big snake) there. Soon a crowd gathered, with pitchforks, boat-hooks, hoes, axes, and two double-barreled guns. Several shots were fired at it. It disgorged three fowls. I missed my cats, and began looking for them; but they were not to be found. The men skinned the snake,—they always skin them,—and when they cut it there were my two cats. The snake was a boa-constrictor, just eleven feet long. People who eat them say they are as sweet as pork. Rats are also eaten by many of the people. Bats are quite a luxury,—not the small bats you have in America. These are much larger. Mr. Flickinger has a cap made from bat-skins.

We have one little boy in the mission by the name of Scipio Africanus. He is just forty-five inches high. In the Sabbath-school he is in the infant class, taught by Sister Betty Caulker. He often comes to tell me what his teacher tells the class. He gets his English fearfully mixed up. A few Sabbaths ago he told me, " Yeam [mammy] Betty been say dat time when Jesus been born persons been there for mind sheep and koolang [goats]. One angel came to um. He shine like sun. Dem people 'fraid de angel; so he tell um, 'No for 'fraid; I no go hurt you. I come for bring you good news.' That time there been some people come out far country. Them ask the king which side Jesus dere. Dat time when he been born him mammy put him in dat place where dem cow can eat." This little boy has a wonderful memory, and is very fond of learning. He says he wants to see his mother, but he wants to know book first.

All our children who were carried off by the Purrow-devil are back again. Their backs and breasts are cut in the regular heathen style. At first some of them tried to hide it from me.

JOSEPH GOMER.

INDUSTRIAL SCHOOL IN AFRICA.

You ask for my plans about the industrial school, or farm. I propose to push it, and make it pay for the keeping of every child. That is all I am aiming at. We are not well fixed yet, but we are making all our own palm-oil; and when it rains so that the children can not work on the farm I have them cracking palm-nuts. We sell the kernels at five shillings per bushel, in cash. My next report will show a few shillings for kernels; and when we get fixed we will make palm-oil soap, and sell it. Next dry season I shall sell some arrowroot and some ginger; also, some cassava. We have sold some cassava already. Everything on the farm looks well, except the corn and cotton. I do not count much on them this year, but I shall not give them up. We shall get some cotton. I have sent a sample to England, to see what it is worth there. Our children are living almost altogether on farm-products—cassava and sweet-potatoes. We have a good lot of sweet-potatoes.

I am now setting hedge-fence,—setting posts and tying palings to them to protect the hedge until it grows. I am planting the Bahama-grass for pasture. I shall keep sheep and cows as soon as the fences are completed. I keep a watchman now, who carries a gun, and looks after things generally at night. The leopards are still very numerous.

I think you need have no fears about the industrial farm being a failure. How long does it take to get a farm so that it pays in America, where you have practical farmers, and horses and oxen that are broken to work, and no one to humbug you. JOSEPH GOMER.

July 13, 1878.

MR. GOMER'S APPEAL TO SUNDAY-SCHOOLS.

As for opening new schools, I shall not open any until I am fully persuaded that it is right to do so.

I can not understand why it is that so many of the Sabbath-schools in America are so fearful to undertake to support a school here. They should give their money and their prayers at the same time; and if they have faith like old Granny Aunt Kate—the old lady received into the church here at dedication—they would have no fears. She is over eighty years old, and walks out to Flickinger Chapel and attends the six o'clock Sabbath-morning class. It is a wonder how she gets her living; yet she always wears a smile, and seems to trust God for everything.

But perhaps the people fear they will not be able to raise the money. Did not Dr. Cullis—one man—buy grounds and put up a very large hospital in Boston, on faith,—by trusting God for the money? Will not God perform all that he has promised? I believe it to be sin not to trust him.

But I am not complaining. The people have done nobly for Africa. Did not the good people about Otterbein Station and Green Hill send a good lot of nice clothes for our poor, naked children? The good people at Westerville also sent their full share of clothing; and before they are all gone we get another good supply of nice, ready-made clothing, for both girls and boys, made to fit as nicely as though a tailor had taken the measure. Surely, God is helping us right along. Then why not trust him? Last Sabbath I dressed up two little boys, from the Lewisburg clothes, and they were the happiest little fellows you ever saw. Surely, these Christians have made unto themselves friends of the mammon of unrighteousness. It is the privilege—I had nearly said the duty—of many others to follow the glorious example set by these good people. And when they fail they would be astonished to see some of the descendants of Ham standing on the shining shore and bidding them a hearty welcome.

But I must close. I wish you could send a good man and his wife out here, he to manage the farm and his wife to have charge of the children; then I could put in all my time laboring among the people in the villages. There should be some one to visit them in their homes. Our itinerants

just visit them on Sunday, and spend only an hour at each place. They can not do justice to the cause. JOSEPH GOMER.
July 17, 1878.

REV. DANIEL F. WILBERFORCE.

This is the boy who came from Africa in the spring of 1871, entered school in Dayton in December of the same year, graduated from its high-school with special honor in June, 1878, became a minister and a member of Miami Conference in August, was married to Miss Lizzie Harris of Dayton, October 17th, and with his wife sailed from New York in the brig Liberia for his native land November 6th, 1878. Early in the year 1872, after being in Dayton but a few months, he became a Christian and a member of the United Brethren Church, of which he is now a missionary. Mr. and Mrs. Wilberforce were happily converted to God, became members of the Third United Brethren Church,—he in 1872 and she previously,—and at its altar they were married, and from its communion they went forth to their far-distant field of labor.

Mr. Wilberforce, while in New York, wrote a letter, from which we extract the following:

Our trip to New York was made pleasant in many ways. In the first place, the conductor

REV D F WILBERFORCE AND WIFE.

with whom we left Dayton looked after us kindly. He not only introduced us to several persons on board the train, but when the train stopped for supper he took us into the dining-hall and paid for our suppers. We were much surprised at this, for it is not often that we find conductors so ready to oblige; and we wondered, too, how he knew us and all about our future work. He was not only kind to us, but he had a pleasant smile for everybody who spoke to him.

On the train was Dr. Hoyt, editor of the *Western Christian Advocate*, from Cincinnati, on his way to New York. He dropped in a pleasant word here and there, and gave me a pamphlet to read.

We traveled all Wednesday afternoon and night, and reached New York City late on Thursday night. But Mr. Flickinger was at the depot to meet us, and I was very glad to see him. It would have been almost impossible for us to get along without him, for a boarding-place had to be secured.

By the way, the prejudice against color has not been taken out of the minds of the people, particularly in this city. New York, with all its educational facilities, its many churches, its talented ministry,—yes, metropolitan New York,— needs missionaries to enlighten its people. We find every kitchen, dining-room,—in short, every place,—filled with colored servants; but when Mr. Flickinger made application for our accommodation, out of four hotels there were none that that could keep us.

We are in a private boarding-house kept by a colored man. We like the place, and would rather stay here than in a hotel; but it is a long distance from the business part of the city. Mr. Flickinger came on Saturday evening to board with us, as he preferred to be with us while we were in the city. He is still boarding with us. I believe he eats as much, walks as fast, does his business as well, sleeps as sound,—even though he boards in a house owned and kept by a colored man, and eats at a table surrounded by colored people.

We finished our work of preparation at 4:00 P. M. to-day, when Mr. Flickinger said, "Now, I can make the 5:30 train;" and he did. We have orders to be aboard at 9:00 A. M. to-morrow, and if all goes well we will be out of sight of land twenty-four hours hence. Truly, we have much to thank the Lord for, as well as the good people of Dayton and elsewhere, and especially I, who have been snatched from the degradation of heathenism through their kind interposition.

GOOD NEWS FROM AFRICA.

Mr. Wilberforce and wife landed in Freetown, West Africa, December 17th, after a voyage of forty days from New York. They suffered but little with sea-sickness, and were in good health and spirits when they landed. Mr. and Mrs. Gomer, who had been in Freetown several days awaiting their arrival, accompanied them to Shengay on the 23d. Mr. Gomer says of the condition of the work:

In all of our stations where we have held meetings or taught school—Otterbein excepted—the hand of God has been manifest. Meetings have been held every Sabbath, with few exceptions, at Shooney, Senehoo, Kattah, and Tissannah, villages near Shengay, and at Thumbah, Bendoo, Bouthe, Tiama, and Manoh, also at Senehoo, Bowmah, and Tissannah, near Bomphetook. Bro. Hero has held meetings occasionally at Martin, Moyah, and Mo Carmo, near Mambo.

At Shengay the meetings have not been as well attended as we could wish; yet there has been a good interest in the seekers' meeting, held Sunday morning at six o'clock. Fourteen from it have been received into the Church, nine of whom were mission-boys. There are still twenty-three names on the seekers' class-book. The average attendance at the Sunday-school is about seventy, and at the day-school about forty. We have now in the industrial school nineteen boys and five girls.

The meetings at Otterbein Station have not been well attended.

At Senehoo and Bowmah, near here, the meetings are encouraging. The average attendance at the day-school is only eighteen.

The work at Manoh Station is very encouraging Mrs. Curtis, the teacher, has a large seekers' class. There are four whom she believes are converted. One is the head-man of the town, two others are among the chief men, and the fourth is an old woman. I visited the school a few weeks ago. There were twenty-six children in attendance; but Mrs. Curtis says that several of them do not attend regularly. She also teaches a night-school for adults, with an attendance of from twenty to thirty-five.

We have a good start at Thumbah Station. The chief, Kong Cottle, is a fine man, and encourages the work. He attends the meetings regularly when at home. There is a regular daily attendance at the school of fourteen scholars—all boys.

We are truly thankful to God for the prospects at Mambo.

ANOTHER LETTER FROM SHENGAY.

Rev. J. B. Elliott, manager of Western District, in the colony of Sierra Leone, was twice called to go to Shengay in the month of October, 1878, While there he wrote the following to our treasurer, Rev. J. K. Billheimer. The letter is dated Shengay, October 7th.

From the above you will see where I am while writing this, and will be pleased to hear something of the place where you once labored and suffered much. The seed was not sown in vain, nor are your labors as the pioneer of your missionary society unrewarded.

What a great contrast, when comparing the past with the present. Now you have first-rate day-schools and Sabbath-schools equal to any at Freetown, Bible and other classes well attended, church-services well crowded with anxious worshipers, and an industrial school in good working order.

There are very good cassava, corn, and potato farms, growing beautifully, worked partly by the children before and after school. I was wonderfully surprised at the answers the children gave to the questions in geography, grammar, and arithmetic.

I preached to a crowded assembly in the church

yesterday morning and on a night previous, through an interpreter.

Brother and Sister Gomer work very hard, without complaining or making any fuss. Punctuality and economy are strictly carried out; and without doubt they are the hardest-working missionaries I have yet known. I wish you had many such whom you could send over here.

MORE WORK FOR CHRIST.

I have been very busy since my arrival, and things are going on nicely here. More work for Christ is our motto. We ought to open another station soon. You must not disappoint us. I want one in the Cockborough River country soon. Let the Redeemer's kingdom extend. Let no consideration of dollars and cents hinder the progress of our work. I visited Tom Tucker's town. He wants a school there; the people also desire a school. You know Tom is really headman of the place; and he calls himself an American, therefore his town must be ours. I took the small boat the other day and went to look at the place. The people received me gladly. At night I held services, and there were upward of forty present. The people were very attentive. This was the first meeting ever held in the place. It was somewhat amusing, when we knelt to pray, to hear those who had caught the idea, calling to the others to kneel. Of course all through the congregation they were calling upon each other. Quiet must be restored before we could proceed; but those who were trying to quiet the others made so much noise doing it that it was just as bad. The people thanked us very kindly. When we were about to leave that night they gathered on the bank, uttering their regrets at parting. And so affected was I by this mark of God's favor on my work that evening that I resolved by his grace to do something for this people. I can not bear the thought that they must die in their present condition. Let us have a school here. Let us win the country for Christ. Tom Tucker's people must be saved. We owe a debt to Tom that has never been paid. More than all, we owe humanity, we owe God, a debt that must be paid, or he will call us shortly to account. Tom Tucker's town for God! should ring forth as the watch-word from every Sabbath-school in the land. Had I the power I would write in flaming characters these words. I would write them over every pulpit, in every Sunday-school. I would point to them continually, until every one would be made to feel as did Belshazzar before the handwriting on the wall in the Babylonian palace. Some Sabbath-school ought to respond at once. Now let us have immediate response. Let not one school wait for another. Ever yours.

DANIEL F. WILBERFORCE.

Freetown, West Africa, April, 1879.

THOMAS TUCKER.

Thomas Tucker was picked up on Sherbro Island, twenty-five years ago. His heathen or "country" name was "Tong."

Tong was a genuine heathen boy, without learning, not only not knowing the first letter of the alphabet, but not knowing that such a thing existed. He soon became interested in the mission-work, and proved himself a truthful and devoted servant. There are in the character of Thomas Tucker several elements that are not common. One is honesty; another, gratitude; and another, humility.

In Africa, Christianity means elevation, removal from a lower to a higher position or station in life. As this does not come as the result of merit, either entailed or acquired, but from the unselfish labors of Christian men and women, one would naturally look for gratitude, at least; and when we fail to find honesty, humility, and gratitude,— as is too often the case,—it is discouraging.

What used to be Tong, the ignorant heathen

SAW MILL.

TOM TUCKER.

boy, is now Thomas, the enlightened Christian man. He is a home evangelist, a kind of local preacher, without quarterly or annual conference license. He speaks the Sherbro dialect.

"A SIDE-DOOR."

We have also entered at a small side-door, so to speak. This door was unlocked in 1857, and for more than twenty years it has been standing open night and day. It opens to us a field—not a harvest-field of ripe grain ready for the reaper, but a field all covered with a dense growth of the vilest passions, the darkest deeds, and the grossest superstitions of which the lowest order of mind is capable—waiting for the sharp-edged sword of the Spirit to clear the ground and prepare it for the seed of the word of God.

Sherbro Mission has already assumed proportions of no mean dimensions. Twenty-two years ago a little fire was kindled on the western shores of upper Sherbro. At first it burned slowly, and threw a very faint light against the dark background of heathen life. At one time the fire came very near going out; and but for an over-ruling Providence it would have gone out. Deep and important interests were placed in the balances at the sixteenth session of this Board, and at the General Conference at Lebanon, Pennsylvania, which made them quiver. Had the interests of this mission been left entirely to the wisdom of men, it would have been abandoned; but God himself came to the rescue and saved to the Church this important field.

J. K. BILLHEIMER.

February, 1879.

LETTER FROM MRS. GOMER.

My health is not the best. The house-work in the mission, with nine heathen children, is no easy task. No person but those who have been placed in the same situation can form the slightest idea of the amount of patience required. My Lewisburg class of seven little girls has grown to fifteen or twenty. There are some little boys in it; and it is no use to try to send them away. I teach them in Thomas Caulker's gate-house. You know how it is arranged. Last Sabbath, just after service commenced in Flickinger Chapel,—which was well filled,—a woman with her babe went and sat on the front steps. A snake came and bit her on the foot. She screamed, and nearly all the people left the church. They killed the snake. For several hours the woman was in great pain, but she will recover.

M. W. GOMER.

Freetown, West Africa, May 10, 1879.

LETTER FROM MR. WILBERFORCE.

I found my people at Bonthe, British Sherbro, my birthplace, all well. Father, mother, and sisters wept when they saw me. They had almost given up the hope of ever seeing me at home; and now that they saw me with their own eyes their joy was unbounded. When my father heard I was coming home from America—I wrote just as we were leaving New York—he began preparations for a grand dinner. A few days after my arrival the dinner was given. There were killed many fowls and ducks, and two pigs. We had a grand time. The mission-house was used for the missionaries and those of my friends who had been my former school-mates. The country people and others preferred to have their dinner at my sister's house. With plenty of rice and soup, there was nothing that could mar the enjoyment of my country relatives. Father gave me a sheep, and I took it to Shengay. It was quite a pet. I called it "Dick." It was a pet with all the mission-children. Not long ago I went to visit my uncle, and while I was gone poor "Dick" sickened and died. Mr. Gomer ordered the men to throw the sheep into the sea, but instead they took it to Shengay, and I suppose had a grand feast. You know everything possible is eaten here—snakes, rats, and things that make one almost sick to mention. When you came to Africa last, you went to see my father. My uncle was there at the time. He has a vast territory, about half a day's walk from Avery Station, Mendi Mission. When I went there uncle was not at home; but I met with a hearty reception. Across the river from my uncle's place is the site of my grandmother's town. The people asked me if I had come to rebuild the town. I said no, not just then, because my work for the present was at Shengay. They seemed very much disappointed. I am the only boy left in our family, and to me they look to rebuild the place. I pray God the time may come when I shall be able to do something for them. My uncle is getting old. He is in religion a Mohammedan. Our family is called a Mohammedan family. But for the grace of God, I too might this day be calling on the Prophet Mohammed. I never said anything while in America of my family, or of the place that properly belongs to us. To be an African chief is no honor. I do not see any of the chiefs here whose position can be envied. A man in authority here might do very much for the extension of the Redeemer's kingdom, and thus bring credit to himself and honor to his God. The country in which my uncle lives is an excellent one. A saw-mill might be built there with fair prospect. Mr. Burton years ago tried to get the place, but one of my uncles, now dead, refused.

At my uncle's place they have some cows, and he gave me one. While I was there I remarked that we use our cattle to plow our fields, instead of having them run about through the town as theirs were doing. The people who heard me wondered how oxen could be made to plow the ground. Some suggested that they used the feet in plowing; others advanced ideas as ridiculous. Finally, I told them that we had one big, big hoe (plow); that the oxen were tied to this, and the man holding the hoe walked behind them, while the big hoe dug its way through the ground. Their surprise was unbounded. Clapping their hands over their mouths, they exclaimed, "*Ah! a-po-tho! a-po-tho!*" (Ah! white people! white people!)

I am glad to say that the meetings are still interesting, though on account of the rains they are not so largely attended as formerly. Our class-meeting was very good last week; though the night was dark, many came. On Thursday night we had a rousing prayer-meeting. The Spirit of God was there. It is not often we have such meetings here. Our people are just taking hold of truth and righteousness—not as rich in experience as those in Christian lands. We are striving to impress the true ideas of civilization both by word and example. We want to stir up more interest among the young people. To do this we had a debate last night on the subject, "From whom has mankind received the most benefit, the agriculturist or the merchant." Both sides were well argued. It was quite an enjoyable time. We ought to have a small printing-press here, and a monthly paper edited by the missionaries. At any rate, we should have a press.

DANIEL F. WILBERFORCE.

Sherbro Mission, West Africa, May 19, 1879.

CHIEF GEORGE CAULKER.

Mr. Caulker is not an ordinary chief of a town; his jurisdiction and authority extend over a large part of the Sherbro country of west Africa. He succeeded his father, the late Thomas Stephen Caulker, chief of the Plantains, Shengay, etc., and at his instance signed the deed of conveyance to the missionary society of the lands now known as Shengay Station.

When a young man his father sent George to England, where he received a fair education, and in this respect has a great advantage over his fellow-chiefs. Having a good understanding of the English language, as well as a perfect knowledge of the Sherbro dialect, he makes one of the most

CHIEF GEORGE CAULKER.

MRS. LUCY CAULKER CURTIS.

efficient interpreters we can find; and we are glad to say he very frequently attends the Sabbath-services at Shengay, interpreting the scripture lessons and sermons, though not a Christian himself. He was our interpreter at the dedication of Bomphetook Chapel, at which time there was read the sixth chapter of II. Chronicles—part of it before and the balance after the sermon. This was not only ably interpreted by Mr. Caulker, but so impressed was he by Solomon's grand utterances in that prayer, by which the temple was consecrated, that he had much to say of its beauty and power afterward. He was frequently deeply affected by the truth of God, and during his last illness prayed much.

He died September, 1881, and his brother, Thomas Neal Caulker, became chief.

LUCY CAULKER CURTIS.

Mrs. Curtis is one of our teachers in Africa. Lucy is one of the numerous daughters of old King Caulker. She was one of the first to come to our school at Shengay, and was one of the three first converts. She was at a verly early age given to a white trader as a "country wife." Against this she protested, although it was usually considered a great honor. We missed her from the mission-school and the inquirer's class.

She had gone, and was living a life of sin. Was it her sin, or that of her father? With Lucy the separation from the man who was called her husband was only a question of time. Heathen children are taught to obey their parents, not only while they are children, but after they have grown up to manhood and womanhood. Lucy patiently submitted to her condition while her father lived. Shortly after his death she insisted on being married according to English law to the man with whom she had lived, and thus legitimize their children, or she would separate from him. This he refused to do, and she at once left him. During all these years of trial Lucy kept her Bible near her, and did not forget the lessons taught her at the mission. She returned to Shengay and built herself a house midway between the town and the mission-station, thus becoming a kind of link between her heathen people and a Christian mission.

Lucy has for some years been employed by the mission as a teacher and helper in our general missionary work in Africa. Her relation to the people, owing to her birth, and her firm stand for the principles of Christianity have given her great influence among the Sherbro people. For some time she has had charge of Manoh Station, about ten miles distant from Shengay, where she teaches, and conducts prayer-meetings. She also has a Sabbath-school, and is under God doing an excellent work at Manoh.

CANNIBALS AND IDOLATORS.

One year ago the people would kill and eat each other at Yondoo, Bomba, and Bacooh. They would disguise themselves in leopard-skins, with iron claws on their hands. They would watch for their prey and spring upon it. Brother Flickinger has a set of these iron claws, which were taken from one of these cannibals, who was caught by the king. A few months ago the native Christians at Shengay organized a native missionary society, to send the gospel to these poor people. The messengers of peace, who have been sent from time to time, have been received with open arms at all these villages. The meetings are well attended; and now they say they want a missionary to come and sit down there— to remain among them. The object of this new aid-society is to employ one man, to travel a large circuit, to read the Bible, preach, and talk about the Christian religion to many people. They have not the means to employ a permanent teacher there. My object in writing this article is to beg the Christians of America—some church, Sabbath-school, or conference,—to send $100,

$150, or $200 a year to support a school-teacher there. It ought to be $200, in order that we may place a good man there.

At Mambo, four years ago, the people were worshiping a pile of bones under some trees in the midst of the town. No new bones have been placed there since the Summit-street Sabbath-school teacher and preacher has been there. Just such a man ought to be at Yondoo. The young man who first pointed out these bones, and explained their use to me, told me that a few years before, when very sick, he had been brought there, and a sacrifice made to them for his recovery. A missionary showed him a better way. When Brother Flickinger was here he gave this same young man some hymn-books to hold service with, in the village where he lives, which I hear he does regularly every Sabbath-day.

J. GOMER.

West Africa, April 3, 1880.

A SURPRISE.

I arrived here the 9th inst., and yesterday morning, as the bells were ringing for church, I looked out of the window, and who should I see coming up the street but Brother Flickinger, who had just landed. I thanked God in my heart. If his last visit here was hailed with delight, this is doubly so; for there are many things to be done

MRS. M. M. MAIR.

here that no one else could well do. Surely his coming at this time is most providential. Churches and schools must have his counsel. And then there is a new project on foot, of which you shall hear more hereafter. JOSEPH GOMER.

Freetown, Sierre Leone, January 12, 1880.

FIRST VISIT TO ROTUFUNK.

Though I have been in Africa this time only ten days, I have traveled over two hundred miles in a row-boat, going to Rotufunk with Mr. Gomer. We saw quite a number of alligators, naked people, mangrove swamps, and some beautiful country. Our business was to see Chief Richard Caulker and others in authority there, to obtain from them a site for the Woman's Missionary Association buildings, near the town of Rotufunk. We met the chief in his canoe, on the Bomphe River, some eight or ten miles this side of Rotufunk, about eleven o'clock Thursday night, and told him our business. He assured us he would meet us the next day at noon; but it was night before we saw him, and then we walked a mile and a half over a rough road to find him. Mrs. Mary M. Mair, who is now in charge of the woman's mission in Africa, Rev. Joseph Gomer, superintendent of Sherbro Mission, and two boatmen,—who carried Mrs. Mair and ourself across a very muddy, snaggy swamp, with water in it three feet deep,—made up the company that called upon Mr. Caulker. He agreed to be ready to accompany us next day to Mamoo, where the other chiefs were, which he did,—we taking him and three other dignitaries in our own boat.

We had come only a short distance when we met a man paddling a canoe up the river. He called out to Mr. Caulker that one of his wives had "born him a picken" in the next town. He asked what time, and what it was; and after being told, he slowly said over these words, as though he wished to fix them well in his memory: "A boy, 5 o'clock in the morning, January 17th, 1880." We soon passed that town, but he said nothing about stopping to see his son. We we were glad of it, for we had to stop farther along, to see a Mr. Coker. Mr. Caulker has two wives in this town. He has two at Sammoh, where he joined us that morning, two at Bomphe, where Mr. Coker lives, two at Mamoo, where our meeting was held, and how many where the "picken" was born, and in other places, we did not learn. We landed at Mamoo at 9 o'clock and left at 4, with the paper, properly signed by Mr. Caulker and four others, giving the Woman's Missionary Association at Rotufunk the use of one hundred acres of ground for ninety-nine years. Our meeting in Mamoo was in the barra in the center of the town. The next house to it on one side was occupied by the finest-looking cow and calf I have seen in this part of Africa. Asking if I could buy them, the head-man said, with emphasis, "No." I next asked if I could buy some bananas or rice there. The reply was, "Nothing for sell. Too much hungry live in this country." We then asked why they did not raise plenty of rice, and cattle, and everything, as they had rich land, and good grass for cattle and horses, and ought to have plenty of food to eat and to sell. With a sad look the head-man, who is reported as being a very good heathen ruler, said, "Too much war live here. If we work and get anything, war come and spoil our town."

Rum and war—and the first makes most of the latter—are great evils in Africa; and, be it said to our shame, white people will continue to send rum here. And in not a few instances the white traders of this country instigate war, which is often carried on for no other purpose than plunder. Working and getting food and stock and other valuable things about them is to invite war to their town. Rather than to have that, they grow so little that they often suffer with hunger themselves. The numerous vices introduced here by white men, added to the many already existing among the natives, have fearfully degraded, yea, well-nigh destroyed, the people of western Africa.

Shengay, West Africa, January 21, 1880.

FUNERALS IN AFRICA.

I want the people of America to know what a mournful sight a heathen funeral is, that they may the better sympathize with these poor people. Surely no people ever needed the gospel and the prayers of Christians more than these people. I am just from the town of Shengay, where they are having a mammoth "funeral cry." About two weeks ago there was brought to Shengay, from a village away up one of the rivers, a woman who was very sick. Brothers Flickinger and Wilberforce and myself called on her one night, but she was past speaking. Brother Wilberforce asked if she had ever prayed. They replied that she was not able. That night she died, and at once the "cry" began. Loud cries, sobs, yells, and bitter moans are heard, and drums and other musical instruments are brought into use. All relatives and friends, and even strangers, are expected to join in the cry. On entering the hut where the corpse is, the criers kneel or prostrate themselves on the ground, sometimes embracing the corpse, at the same time weeping, sobbing, and uttering the most bitter cries. Per-

sons who will not join in the cry are considered
not to be friends; but as a rule there is no want
of criers, for the relatives of the deceased person
must supply drink, which usually consists of rum,
gin, or palm-wine. Where the friends are able
all of these are provided, and food also for persons from distant villages. The crying is kept
up night and day as long as drink is supplied.
This woman died Tuesday night. On Thursday
she was taken to Tassoh, three miles distant, for
interment. She was carried by four men, who
were frequently relieved by others. On arriving
at Tassoh, a small present is made to the head-
man of the village, and he consents to the interment. The grave is then dug. By this time the
mourners arrive, and the coffin is lowered into
the grave. And now begins another indescribable
scene of bidding the corpse good-by and of sending messages to departed friends,—such as "Tell
daddy how do," or "Tell mammy how do." Some
very strange messages are sent to the other world.
The crying at this point is most distressing. After
the grave is filled up the mourners throw themselves on it and roll in the dirt. The party now
return to Shengay, and continue crying, drumming, dancing, and firing guns all night. Many
of the more civilized people in Shengay complain they can not sleep. The chief, George

Caulker, is not at home, and most of these people are strangers. JOSEPH GOMER.

Mission-House, Shengay, W. A., January 24, 1880.

MAMBO MISSION-STATION.

Mr. Hero had been told that we were coming to organize a church; and he thought that there were twenty-eight names, out of fifty-two that he had in his book as believers in and seekers of Christ, which ought to go upon a class-book. Among these were the head-man and the most influential citizens of Mambo. We told him that none who were connected with the liquor-traffic, or held slaves, or practiced polygamy, or were members of the Purrow Society, could be taken into the organization. He had gone over the list of names several times, and each time the number was reduced. When the fact was fully realized by Mr. Hero and his wife—for Sister Hero as well as her husband had been instrumental in inducing these people to turn from idolatry to God—that slavery and polygamy would keep out of the Church some of their most promising converts, the sadness of their hearts was so visible upon their countenances that we pitied them. They, however, cheerfully acquiesced, and said it was right. They then carefully went over the list again, and gave us the names of twelve persons; and after morning service on the 22d of February these persons were baptized and organized into a church. Mr. and Mrs. Hero's names were also added, making a class of fourteen members at Mambo, with as many more who are worthy of being members as soon as they can free themselves from slavery and polygamy.

ORGANIZATION OF MISSIONARY DISTRICT IN AFRICA.

We did not decide to organize such a district in Africa until within ten days of the time it was done. Our hesitation was mainly caused by the fear that the Church in America would not supply the necessary funds to enable such an organization to prosper as would be expected. There being, besides Brothers Gomer and Wilberforce, four native ministers employed in Africa, none of whom have been tried less than two years, and all of them expressing themselves willing and anxious to continue in the work, we thought it wise to organize a district, which we did March 20th, 1880, the time that was chosen more than a month before for a meeting of all our teachers and missionaries at Shengay to adopt a uniform plan of school-teaching and working generally. Accordingly, Rev. M. Sawyer, in charge of Bomphetook, Rev. J. B. W. Johnson of Bomphe Town, Frank Dixon of Thumbah, and Lucy Curtis

Caulker of Manoh, found their way to Shengay on the 19th, and early next morning Rev. J. P. Hero, from Mambo, arrived. Revs. J. W. Pratt, D. F. Wilberforce, and J. Gomer are employed at Shengay. The latter two and myself being members of Miami Conference, we constituted ourselves an examining committee, before whom Messrs. Sawyer, Johnson, Pratt, and Hero appeared at 7:00 A. M. to answer the questions proposed to applicants for annual-conference membership, as found in our Discipline. By half-past nine o'clock we had our work done, and adjourned to eat breakfast.

We met at the chapel at 11:00 A. M., and, to our surprise, found quite an audience, it having been announced the Sabbath before that all the missionaries intended to meet there for the organization of a mission-district. Not only all of our missionaries and teachers were there, but Mrs. Mair of Rotufunk, and Mr. Johnson, her teacher, also favored us with their presence and counsel. A half-hour was spent in devotional exercises and three hours in business; and truly God was there to help us sing, pray, think, and speak. To use the language of others, "That was a grand time;" "Did not think you could have so good a meeting as that;" "Why, to come to Shengay seems like being in a Christian land." Discussing the questions of how to open a high-school, conduct Sunday-schools, and how to itinerate to the best advantage, etc., "Why, is this Africa or America?" and similar expressions, will indicate the feelings of those present. And really it was good to be there.

ROTUFUNK AND SHENGAY.

I arrived here the morning of the 20th, at four o'clock. Mrs. Mair has been waiting more than two weeks for pine boards to finish sheeting the roof of the new house. She bought country boards on the 21st to finish three sides of the piazza-floor, which the carpenters are working at now, and will complete to-day, I think; and as soon as the sheeting comes the shingling can commence. Mrs. Mair has concluded to have one room finished and move into it, and then dispense with two of the carpenters. She is busy, as usual. Mr. Smith has found plenty of water at forty-two feet, and is walling up the well. The fence is finished, and a little garden is made.

A good prayer-meeting was held in the parlor Thursday night. These meetings, with the daily morning prayers, give to this part of Rotufunk a very civilized aspect. There is no end to the visitors coming and going every day. Where they come from and where they go to is more than I can tell.

All was going well at Shengay. Our corn was planted, and some of it is up. I left them planting arrowroot. Mr. Wilberforce was busy with the school. The chief was at Thumbah, trying to find out who poisoned Chief Cockle.

Last evening we went over to a small village near here, and as I looked at the poverty and wretchedness of the people I thanked God that I was born in a Christian land. The rickety and tumble-down condition of their mud-huts, the great scarcity of clothing among them,— the children having no clothing,—the devil-houses and the train-houses, together with the gregrees, charms, and sabbas worn by the people and hung over their doors, prove that Satan does not waste his time in idleness, but that he has a strong hold upon these people. Some Mohammedans were sitting about on their mats, with their beads, ready to say their prayers just as the sun would drop out of sight in the West. They all sit with their faces to the East, toward Mecca, and bend forward until their foreheads strike the ground. Some have done this so much that there is quite an abrasion on their forehead. They sit on their mats in front of their huts, or in the burra, and pray, looking all about them meanwhile.

We are much encouraged in our work here.

The Lord is with us and for us, and what more can we ask? We have enemies here who would rejoice to see the good work fail; but Jesus is our captain, and he will surely lead us to victory.

JOSEPH GOMER.

Rotufunk, Africa, April 23, 1880.

LETTER FROM MR. WILBERFORCE.

I have just this evening returned from some of my appointments up the Cockborough River. I preached on Saturday evening at M'Caibay, on Sabbath morning at M'Kelleh and Good Hope, and in the evening at Good Hope, making in all four services. A hard rain gave us a good drenching. I reached home wet and hungry, but no worse. The boat will leave for town early in the morning, and I must send you a letter.

You little know how much we missed you after you left Freetown. When you and David went away, it seemed as though we had lost some one.

Mrs. Gomer, Mrs. Wilberforce, and myself are well, but Mr. Gomer has a sore throat that troubles him. I hope you reached home safe and sound together with David, and found all well.

D. F. WILBERFORCE,

Shengay, West Africa, May 3, 1880.

SAFE RETURN.

I landed at New York the 6th of May, 1880, after a voyage of thirty-six days, coming from

Africa on a sail-vessel. I left our missionaries there reasonably well, happy, and busy. God is blessing our foreign missions abundantly.

I wish to record my heart-felt gratitude to God for his loving-kindness toward me during the seven months' absence in Germany and Africa, and especially in making the days and nights spent upon the deep waters, which otherwise would have been so lonely and gloomy, to be days and nights of genuine contentment and religious enjoyment; also, for giving me working-health every day I was in Africa, though I did suffer considerably from climatic influences and loss of sleep on account of traveling so much in a row-boat at night. God has prospered our undertakings both in Germany and in Africa far beyond what we had reason to expect, and by his merciful providence kept the intense cold of Germany as well as the great heat and malaria of Africa from permanently harming me. The Lord caused me to realize in a marked manner that his ways are ways of pleasantness, and all his paths are peace.

HAD THEIR OWN RELIGION.

I returned this morning from a trip over to Yondoo. I visited Rembee and Baccah also. I held three meetings at Yondoo, all of which were well attended. At both the other places I had about forty listeners. There was much water in the way. Rembee is a large town, and well deserves a school. It has a very intelligent head-man. At Baccah three Mohammedan women sat on mats in a yard opposite where I held the meeting, which took place in the open air, I standing in the shade of a house. As these women were looking through the gate and watching me, I told the head-man to invite them over. He said they could not come. I sent Alexander, my interpreter, to ask them to come over, and they brought their mats and sat down in the street and heard me through. One of them then came to thank me. I asked her if she was pleased with what I had said. She said no; that she had her own religion, which she liked better.

Everything at Shengay is about as you left it. I went to Bomphetook and ordered the school stopped because the people would not repair the barra. The whole town turned out at once and repaired it, and the school goes on. The tornadoes have been severe this season. They nearly stripped the mission-house at Bomphetook and made fearful work with the boys' home and the laborers' houses here. The farm is coming on nicely. The oxen have been sick, but are now well. JOSEPH GOMER.

Shengay, West Africa, June 17, 1880.

LETTER FROM AFRICA.

Yours of May 6th was received yesterday, on my return from a trip to Yondoo, Rembee, and Barkoh. I have not forgotten what a time you and I had that day we started for Yondoo but failed to get there, and had to spend several hours under a scorching sun, on a small, treeless island, out in the middle of the bay. I have taken good care ever since to start in time, and to push my crew, and have not since had the pleasure (?) of a day on Porbarlot banks. We praise God for your safe arrival home.

I see so many openings that God has made in answer to the prayers of the Christian church. To undertake a work of such magnitude is certainly a great work, and must be arduous, and the sum of money required enormous; but then we can not now back out of our engagement. We gave our word as a church, and we must abide by it. We must not be as the colored brother who went into the field to pray, saying, "O Lord, look on this poor niggah. Ise done tired libbin' in dis world; Ise ready to go; do, Lord, take poor niggah home;" and when it began to thunder, and the lightning to flash, he became frightened at what seemed a certain answer to his prayer, and cried as he ran away, "O Lord don't do it; Ise jes' been foolin'." God has opened a vast territory, into which the church must march and possess the land. But can we, after having entered into sacred covenant with Him, now become frightened at the answer he has sent, and fall back? God forbid!

The rains are unusually heavy this season. But we can not halt till the Master gives the command. The marching-order, "Go forward!" has flashed across the lines, and "Forward!" should be the cry from every officer in Christ's army.

DANIEL F. WILBERFORCE.

Shengay, West Africa, June 29, 1880.

PREACH FIVE TIMES A DAY.

It affords me pleasure to write an acknowledgment of the receipt of your letter, written June 17th. I am sure your return from Africa to America will create joy in the hearts of all who take deep interest in the work of missions. The boy Bail Moore, who got your name, begs to be kindly remembered to you. I visit and preach in all the towns near me once every Sunday. In fact, I preach five times every Sunday when the weather permits. The more distant towns I visit every fortnight.
J. P. HERO.

GREAT CHANGES TAKEN PLACE.

Great changes have taken place in this part of Africa within a few years, both in the educational and religious departments. When I left Africa in 1871, Freetown was then the educational and religious center. Even then there were but very few institutions that could teach anything higher than that afforded in the ordinary mission-schools. Now there are four institutions that are teaching the higher branches of education,—English and classical. Many of Africa's sons and daughters are now seen crowding into the temple of learning.

And assuredly does the progress of religion keep pace with the march of education; for as the youths become better educated the pulpits become better supplied. Ministers, who before could hardly read the Scriptures, are now replaced by young men who are quite efficient in interpreting the word and explaining the "unsearchable riches of Christ."

The greatest progress thus far made by any church has been made by the mission at Shengay. Less than ten years ago this mission had no name whereof to boast. Indeed, it was a question whether the work of this mission should be continued. Many hearts were discouraged; the faith of many was dim. There was but one poor station, struggling with strong forces that sought its overthrow. Now, instead of one, there are four principal stations where there are held regular

preaching-services and teaching. From these four stations as centers, the word of God goes out to more than forty villages and towns, far and near. From these various improvements in education and religion, I am justified in saying that we stand upon the threshold of another era in the history of Africa. From various quarters the cry for the gospel comes. Many eyes are turned to us for help. DANIEL F. WILBERFORCE.
Shengay Mission, July 31, 1880.

WONDERFUL SUCCESS.

Last Sabbath I was at Bomphetook. Mr. Sawyer is having wonderful success there. We admitted nine persons into full membership and eight as seekers of religion. Many others are almost ready to renounce heathenism. Several of the old members have returned to the station, and several came from the villages where they are living. The people from the villages near are attending meetings well at Manoh and Bomphetook. Those at Bauudah, where we went from Bomphetook, are attended very well. I have three wooden gods, which were brought in lately,—two from villages near Manoh and one from near Rotufunk. Raunchawah, the second head-man at Manoh, brought me all the gregrees and charms out of his house. He has surrendered everything now except slaves. Though he owns none, he has promised to pay slaves for debts previously contracted, and the parties will take nothing else. Thus you see Satan's kingdom is tottering, and gradually it is falling to pieces. Mrs. Wilberforce was very sick, and was taken to town to a doctor. My wife and myself are having most excellent health now.

JOSEPH GOMER.

Shengay, West Africa, September 22, 1880.

MRS. MARY M. MAIR.

We have a most vivid recollection of our first acquaintance with Mrs. Mair. She came to America from Scotland about the year 1854, attended Oberlin College about two years, whence with her husband she went to Africa to join the Mendi Mission. In this field she has for many years been a valuable teacher. She teaches not only the first principles of a common education, but the practical duties and work of life; and not these alone, but that country and people have never had a more faithful and better qualified teacher of God's word than this good woman. Mrs. Mair is a close student of the Bible, apt and always ready to teach the way to heaven. More than one missionary is indebted to her watchful care and tender nursing for the prolongation of life.

Mrs. Mair is now in the employ of the Woman's Missionary Association, and has charge of their station at Rotufunk. She is teacher, and in one sense preacher, lawyer, doctor, housekeeper,—everything necessary to be done in a foreign mission-station. May God grant that the Woman's Missionary Association may long be favored with her services.

SECOND VISIT TO MANOH

Sabbath morning, March 7th, 1880, at 4:00 A. M., Mr. Wilberforce and myself had the boat "Sandusky" and a crew of four men, including one of the mission-boys, in readiness to go to Manoh, which place we reached at eight o'clock. Mrs. Curtis and other missionaries here thought a church ought to be organized there; and we concluded to meet the people and learn their true condition.

Mrs. Curtis had a list of fourteen names, which she said represented persons who came regularly to all the meetings and were living good lives. We reminded her that five things must be absolutely given up by all who became members of the Church; namely, polygamy, slavery, Purrowism, the liquor-trffic, and working on the Sabbath. She said all that had been told them; but she was glad that we had come to tell the people ourselves.

They listened very attentively to our statement; and then the head-man said he had neither slave nor wife, had quit the Purrow, and used no strong drink. The second head-man said he had one wife, and one slave which he holds the same as a sister. She is good, and make farm for him, and they get on nicely. He said our law was good for the children we were training up in the mission-schools, but that they were "only bush people, and no sabbe book," and were old now and could not change well. Another old man said he "gree" with the rules of the Church; they are good, and he would live up to them. Then a younger man said he would also do so; and the head-man's son also agreed to live up to the rules of the Church; only he "no be married right yet, 'cause the girl's mother no gree for that." One woman said she could "gree" to the rules of the Church, only a man owed her some slave-money, and she wanted to get that first, as she "no able to pay him."

We could have organized a small class, but thought it wise not to do so.

ANXIOUS TO HEAR THE GOSPEL.

Yondoo, Rembee, and Barkoh are still alive. Our meetings there are not regular; for we can not always send workers—the sea is too rough and traveling is dangerous. A few weeks ago some young men who had gone to these places to hold meetings when returning had their barge upset, and all the articles it contained were lost. They floated about in the water, clinging to the barge, more than two hours. Some men in a passing canoe finally saw them and picked them up. The people in those tows are arranging to build barras during the coming "dry season." I hope, however, to be able by that time to secure the service of some one to locate there; for it is a field which promises abundant harvest. Mo Harah, M'Kelleh, M'Caibay, and Good Hope were all attended to.

We are compelled to pass by other towns, because we have no time. I think there is enough work for many more. Other stations should be opened, forming centers or starting-points from which the work is to extend.

DANIFL. F. WILBERFORCE.

Shengay, West Africa, August 16, 1880.

AN APPEAL FROM THE DARK CONTINENT.

The organization of a mission-district in Sherbro Mission, West Africa, has not only given us a prestige hitherto unfelt, but has necessarily turned our attention to the subject of giving to the youth of the land a higher Christian education, thus fitting them for work in the Christian ministry. If the church in Africa is to have that rapid and effectual growth which God intends, if the tribes far and near are to be brought to the saving knowledge of God, it can only be done by educating native youths for the work. They must be trained in our own institutions, and made acquainted with our church-polity and doctrine. The United Brethren in Christ must educate their own ministers and teachers. In the past and at the present we may be pardoned for employing men from other societies. But it seems to me that the future standing of this mission can be better secured in the training of its own teachers, instead of going to other sources to look for help. The principles and government of our church would lead us to look to America as the only foreign country where we would wish to have our youth educated. But it must be seen that a plan to educate all our ministers and teachers in that far-off land is not only impracticable, but would little tend to bring about the desired result.

I call upon pastors, superintendents, and Sabbath-schools all to lend a hand to the many poor but promising young men of the land. May the Father of good inspire our hearts to engage more earnestly in this holy service of love, sacrifice, and devotion. DANIEL F. WILBERFORCE.

Freetown, West Africa, September 25, 1880.

WILD HEATHENISM.

Last month, by advice of Dr. Smith, I took a boat expedition for a little change; and where could I find a better place to visit than my dear friends at your mission? I first went to Rotufunk to visit Mrs. Mair, and was very much pleased with what I saw. It is as yet all wild heathenism. But a good beginning has been made. Mrs. Mair is held in high esteem by the entire community; and her influence is at work like the leaven, which can not be without its effect. They were just having their examinations of the schools at Shengay, preparatory to closing for the Christmas holidays; and I was pleased with the interest that Mr. Wilberforce manifested in that part of the work.

I visited the Turtle Islands, in company with Mr. Gomer and Mrs. Mair. That would be an interesting field to occupy. We had services the two evenings I spent there, and the people listened with apparent interest.

D. W. BURTON.

January 9, 1881.

QUARTERLY REPORT.

I now send you our first quarterly report, ending March 31st, 1881. I am happy to report that the work is prospering at most of the stations.

There have been a few accessions to the Church here and at Mambo. Mrs. Evans has been in poor health, but at present she is able to be about. Bro. Evans is hearty, and doing good service. Bro. Wilberforce and wife have been at Rotufunk since February 9th. They are having good health. Mrs. Gomer has been failing in health for some time.

The work here is becoming so very interesting that I do not like to leave it. I hope to be able to do much itinerating this year; and I feel that there are great blessings in store for our African mission. Just let the united prayers of the Church on that side of the ocean go up to our Father in heaven for his blessings to be showered down upon this work and we *are* blessed.

J. GOMER.

Mission-House, Shengay, W. A., April 11, 1881.

LETTER FROM MRS. MAIR.

You will be glad to know that the new stone house, as it is called here, is finished at last. It looks so fine since it was so nicely painted that it has brought new crowds of strangers to admire it. I am kept so busy showing them pictures, etc., that it is hard work to get any writing done.

We had some very heavy rains this season. Our boat had to be hauled up to get a new keel in it. I have just bought a canoe from Mr. Coker, of Bomphe, so we can use it for itinerating; and it will have to be used at once, to fetch mangrove posts to build a good boat-shed on the bank, on a convenient spot selected by D. F. Wilberforce when he was keeping the place for me while I was resting in Sierra Leone. So you see there is and always will be expensive work going on here.

Chief R. C. Caulker has been off in the Bargroo country for six months.

M. M. MAIR.

Rotufunk, West Africa, July 26, 1881.

DAILY LIFE IN WEST AFRICA.

I was visiting some of our members, among them a man by the name of Hompi Tombana. He was converted last January, and joined the Church in March. He has a wife and three children. He belongs to the chief, and is a quiet, good man. He was once employed in this mission. Yeama-Ki, a sick woman, was in the same house with Hompi. She was glad I had come back from Freetown. She was afraid she would die before I returned. She wants me to talk over her when she is dead. She is quite ready to die; for she knows Jesus will take her. All her hope lives upon Jesus.

In going my rounds I came upon a party of six or eight men who seemed to be in trouble.

On inquiring I learned that a very old Timmine woman had died, and that they were not able to bury her. She possessed a Timmine medicine. Demen is the name of it. This medicine must be thrown on her before they could bury her; and as no one there knew the medicine, they had sent away thirty miles to bring a woman who knew the very medicine. The woman had come, but demanded one head of money and eight pieces of cloth before she would pull the medicine. They had got part; but how or where to get the rest was troubling them. They believed that if they were to put hands on the dead woman before she was washed in this medicine the medicine would catch them and they would die. I asked to see the woman. The medicine-woman led me to the hut where the corpse had lain for two days. I pulled the mat to one side and went in, the people watching to see if anything would happen to me.

Matthew Will paid six pieces of cloth for Sateah for a wife for himself. After a couple of years she left him and went to be a wife for Beah. Matthew said, "It is all right. I shall not have to give her cloths. She has carried away two blankets and my shirt and jumper. But never mind; God will give me more." Will sold his house for £2 10s. There were cassava and plantains planted near the house. Yesterday Sateah came to Rev. Mr. Wilberforce to have him make Will give her half the plantains. He brought the case to me; and after hearing both sides, we decided that Sateah had wantonly and wickedly forsaken her husband, and had no right to any of his property. She left apparently quite satisfied. I asked Will what he would do now, as his wife had left him. He said his brother at Shooney was going to send him a wife that would stay with him until he dies.

I went very early to a small town to hold a meeting. The people were not up. I called up the head-man, who assembled all the people. When I had finished speaking I asked if any one had anything to say. The head-man rose and said, "You are the big daddy for the country. You get we all. Sunday we gladdy for that meeting. We like it. Every time you send the meeting to we, we gree for hold um. Only I no get chair. When big man come I like for give him chair or bench self; but I no get. Look to day, you come and I have to spread mat for you. Do Mr. Gomer send me bench, so when you come again I can give you good seat."

J. GOMER.

Shengay, W. A., August, 1881.

EXTRACTS FROM LETTERS.

Nearly all the towns between the Cockborough and Tucker rivers have been visited. Beyond the Cockborough and as far interior as McComboo, and up the mainland, touching Saunno on the Bomphe River, the glad tidings of salvation are heard by the people. I rejoice in the success of the gospel in this territory. You have reason to take courage from the rapid progress made by your work here. God's name be praised. But my heart burns for other towns and people, drawn nearer to me by the strongest ties of nature, that are still beyond this gospel influence.

Brother J. Gomer, in his letter of August 25th, says: "Our king is very sick. On last Friday I went to Mocabby to see him. He said he always prayed; that he was a praying man. I told him that saying prayers is not always praying. I read to him from the Scriptures, and talked and prayed with him. Mrs. Mair was well at last accounts. With reference to our appropriations for the mission, I am afraid we have too much work planned for this year. Soorie Kasebba, Mrs. Mair's chief, is in Freetown. He says he will worship God only; that he can not follow Mohammedans any more. He came here to see the new governor, who is a Christian; and the governor talked good words to him."

Mr. Gomer wrote again, September 10th, eight days after the chief's death, "I was with him three days before his death, and talked and prayed with him, but have no evidence that he was saved. The services were in the barra, where the corpse lay in state. Brother Evans preached the funeral sermon to from three to four hundred people. His brother, Thomas Caulker, who was with the chief when he died, says he has every reason to believe that he was saved, as he constantly asked to be prayed for, and died very easy."

Rev. J. A. Evans wrote the 26th of September, "The country is in an unsettled condition, there being no king or chief chosen yet. Mr. Thomas Neal Caulker is acting chief at present. Saturday and yesterday we held our second quarterly meeting at Shengay for this year. Five persons were received into the Church, and two were baptized. There is a good deal of interest manifested. Brother D. F. Wilberforce is also having some revival at Manoh, where he has lately held a week of prayer, and where Brother Gomer organized a church the other round of quarterly meetings. There are a number of seekers."

SHERBRO MISSION AND ITS WANTS.

[Report made to the Board, May, 1882.]

Shengay, the oldest and principal station of this mission, is located seven and a half degrees north of the equator, and immediately on the coast. Here there are one hundred acres of land belonging to the mission, nearly all of which is cleared and cultivated in coffee, corn, arrowroot, cassava, and other things.

Its buildings consist of a mission-residence and chapel, each thirty by forty-five feet, with stone walls and slate roofs, making them durable. To this residence a frame store-house, with office and bedroom, is attached, which is also of a permanent character. Here are also a number of laborers' houses, tailor, blacksmith, and carpenter shops, the boys' lodging-house and rice-house, all country built, and hence are not very durable; and besides, they must be repaired once or twice every year. Here we have a day-school averaging seventy scholars, and a Sunday-school of one hundred. There are in the industrial school twenty-eight boys and twelve girls. These work about five hours and study four hours each day. Each morning, at 6:00 A. M., they, with laborers and missionaries, spend about one half an hour in worship; then each Tuesday evening there is a

Bible class; Thursday, prayer-meeting; Sunday, at 6:00 A. M., class-meetings; preaching at 11:00 A. M. and 6:00 P. M.; Sunday-school at 2:00 P. M. At all these meetings the mission-children and other citizen children and adults, with laborers, are present. Here there is an organized church.

In a north-eastern direction, about twenty miles from Shengay, is Rembee Station, where we have one hundred and sixty acres of land, a large country-built house, which furnishes room for the schools, preaching, and a place of residence for the missionary. Here we have a good beginning, with only four children in the industrial school and but little land cultivated. But the outlook is quite hopeful. This place was commenced within the last two years. Fifteen miles south from Rembee is Mambo Station. Here we also have one hundred and sixty acres of land, a good country chapel, a small farm opened, nineteen children in the industrial school, and quite a number of other children in both day and Sunday-schools. Here is an organized society. About fifteen miles east from Mambo is Mo Fuss, where we have one hundred and sixty acres of land and no buildings, the station having just been commenced. Twenty miles south from this place is the town of Tongkohloh, where we have also one hundred and sixty acres of land, but nothing else—not even a native missionary. About eighteen miles from here in a north-western direction is Koolong, where we have another tract of land of one hundred and sixty acres, a new frame mission-residence and country-built chapel, twenty-six children in the industrial school, who, with the children supported by their parents and friends, make a good-sized day and Sunday-school. Here there is also an organized church, and the prospects are good. From here north to Shengay it is about fifteen miles more. Between these places is Manoh Station, where we have no land other than that which is occupied by the two country-built houses we have there. Here there are twelve children in the industrial department, day and Sunday-schools, and an organized church, which, though none are large, all are in a flourishing condition. This is not intended to become a regular mission-station, and will be, as it has been, supplied with preaching from Shengay or Koolong. It was commenced, and is now carried forward, by Mrs. Lucy Curtis Caulker, one of our native converts. Mo Fuss is in charge of Thomas Tucker, assisted by Frank Dickson, both of whom are also native converts. In this circle of mission-stations, extending a little over one hundred miles in circumference and within easy reach of them, we now preach in from seventy or eighty towns. This is done by sending out as itinerants a number of native converts and the mechanics which we employ. Our blacksmith, carpenter, tailor, and all are school-teachers—are selected with reference to this. Our day-schools are in operation only four days in the week, giving Saturday, Sunday, and Monday to teachers and pupils, such as can be used, to itinerating. It will also be seen that we now have about one hundred children in the industrial departments. A considerable number of these in the past have become professors of religion, and we hope to see, in time to come, a large per cent of them become Christians. From the ranks of these boys we expect to procure native helpers, who, as school-teachers, itinerants, mechanics, farmers, and boatmen, will render us valuable service in time to come.

The land we have at each of the regular stations will enable us to settle them on lots of from five to ten acres each, and thus keep them under Christian influence and from living in heathen towns.

One of the indispensable things to do to save Africa is to teach her people to develop the resources of that country and thereby obtain the means to procure the things necessary to live civilized Christian lives. Our farming there has already put quite a number to growing coffee and other things which they see can be made profitable to themselves and the country. Our blacksmith, carpenter, and tailor shops are exerting an excellent influence, as may be seen in the fact that more and better clothing is worn, better houses and boats built, more furniture and conveniences in them. It is wonderful how many things are becoming a necessity to the people around our mission-houses, which a few years ago they had no use for at all.

Said Chief Caulker to me the other day,—and in this he represented the sentiments of all the better class of men in that country,—I would not know how to get along without the mission; its schools, shops, farms, stores, and the religious services have become a necessity to my people here. To the Sherbro people it would be like if Americans had to dispense with railway and telegraph lines and daily papers to have no mission now. Our blacksmith and tailor shops do considerable work for them. Our store sells them large quantities of goods. It will not be long until other kinds of business will be in demand there, such as shoe-making, millinery, and dressmaking. We now need at Shengay a good blacksmith, who could play tinner also; a good carpenter, cabinet-maker, and painter; a tailor who could play the cobbler and barber, and a doctor who could practice dentistry, surgery, and mend things generally. Strange as it may seem, it is an important part of mission-work there to teach the people how to farm, how to build and live in houses, how to raise, cook, and eat food, how to make and wear clothing, how to take care of their bodies as well as their souls. If they are to be civilized and Christianized they must be helped out of the small, dirty, cheerless, mud-huts in which they now live. Clothes must be put upon their naked bodies, their food must be eaten from tables instead of sitting on the ground and taking it with their hands out of the vessel in which it was cooked, and they must sleep upon some kind of decent beds instead of on grass-mats as the majority of them now do. To accomplish these things, profitable employment must be given them. They are capable of intellectual, moral, and physical culture, of mastering the most difficult professions and trades, and of becoming good mechanics, doctors, lawyers, preachers, and authors. They love to acquire property, and show real skill in amassing and managing wealth, as a rule, to good advantage. In Freetown many of the most successful merchants, doctors, and ministers are colored men; and the most successful and well-qualified lawyer there is a full-blooded negro and a native African.

The language, "Teaching them to observe all things whatsoever I have commanded," includes the work of teaching them how to live and labor, so that all things may be done decently and in order. "Not slothful in business, fervent in spirit, serving the Lord," is also a divine command, and one based on true reformatory principles. An idle mind may well be called the devil's work-shop. Laziness, nakedness, and filthiness are but other names for wickedness. The apostle declares, yea, commands, "that if any would not work, neither should he eat." There are many things embraced in "all things whatsoever I have commanded you," as these words were spoken by Christ to the successful prosecution of mission-work in western Africa. To do this properly may require, as it did in the case of D. F. Wilberforce, to bring some of these heathen people to America and teach them here. He now, as superintendent of Sherbro mission-schools, presiding elder of that district, and preacher in charge of a large mission, including twenty odd towns, is doing good service for our cause. It is not at all likely that he could have become so efficient a teacher and missionary in twice the length of time in Africa, under the most favorable circumstances, as in the six or seven years spent here.

BOMPHE MISSION.

In former portions of this volume reference is made to Rotufunk and other stations occupied in Africa by the Woman's Missionary Association of the United Brethren Church. Rotufunk, their principal station, is not to exceed thirty miles from Rembee, one of our stations, and is less than fifty miles from Shengay, our head-quarters.

They can easily reach many towns, a number of which are large, from their head-quarters. They have already opened several stations, and are doing an excellent work. Mrs. Mair, the lady in charge of this work, and who is quite a successful missionary, in her last report, made May, 1882, says:

I am glad that my last six-months' account is ready to send to you. My feeble health and the press of work on me at Rotufunk seemed to make the completion of my report impossible.

The month of July, 1881, began with a very disturbed state of the country,—plundering and rumors of wars from far and near. The chief, R. C. B. Caulker, had been absent several months, and the burden of governing the whole Bomphe country was on our head-man, Sourie Kessabie. He called at the mission-house to tell me that he did not know what more to do to preserve peace in the country. He said that the Caulkers on the

Ribbie River were envious because we had built such a fine house in his town, while they had nothing so fine in their part of the Bomphe country. So they were trying to get the young people to "bring war to Rotufunk" to break down our "fine stone house," as they call it, and drive the mission from the country. He wanted me to send for Mr. Gomer, to come from Shengay and help him out of his difficulty. He said that it was Mr. Gomer who got the mission put there at the first, so now he wanted his advice as to what he had better do. I wrote to Shengay, asking Mr. Gomer to come to his aid. Mr. Gomer did not come; but he sent a letter of advice, by the boat. Things began then to get a little more quiet for awhile. We kept going steadily on with our work in the midst of all the commotion and cries of war. The rains were very heavy, and as the roof of the barra leaked, and the mud in and around it was very deep, we were compelled to take our Sabbath-morning service back to the school-house. As there were always crowds of "Timmine" strangers around Kessabie's house and yard I got Mr. Wilson to hold meetings on Sabbath and Thursday afternoons, at five o'clock, in his place. The "Gleaners' Messenger" canoe has been going to many places, carrying missionaries to preach the gospel, through the week as well as on Sabbath.

www.ingramcontent.com/pod-product-compliance
Lightning Source LLC
Chambersburg PA
CBHW030325240426
43673CB00040B/1280